Female diving and dabbl[...]

Red-crested Pochard

Scaup

Tufted Duck

Ferruginous Duck

Goldeneye

Wigeon

Teal

Shoveler

Garganey

Gadwall

Pintail

Mallard

This edition published in 2001 for Bestsellers
Sheffield by Diamond Books an imprint of
HarperCollins*Publishers*
77–85 Fulham Palace Road
London W6 8JB

98 00 02 01 99

2 4 6 8 10 9 7 5 3 1

ISBN: 0 26 167402 1

Originally published in German as a GU Nature Guide by
Gräfe und Unzer GmbH, Munich

© Gräfe und Unzer GmbH, Munich, 1993
© in this English translation HarperCollins*Publishers*, 1994

Written by Jürgen Nicolai, Detlef Singer and Konrad Wothe
Illustrations by Hermann Kacher
This edition translated and adapted by Ian Dawson

Printed and bound in Singapore for Imago

Collins Nature Guide

BIRDS
OF BRITAIN & EUROPE

J. Nicolai ● D. Singer ● K. Wothe

Translated and adapted by
IAN DAWSON

HarperCollins*Publishers*

Bird identification made easy

This new bird guide is designed for nature lovers. Its handy format, the superb colour photos, the informative drawings and distribution maps make it the ideal companion for all who wish to identify birds in their nature expeditions or walks.

There are pictures and descriptions of all the important bird species in Europe.

340 colour photos — taken in the wild — portray the birds with their most important identification characters.
240 drawings of birds show characteristic posture and typical specific behaviour.
320 distribution maps show at a glance where the birds are to be found at any time of year.

Inexperienced observers often make mistakes in identifying birds. Therefore the authors and publishers of this new bird guide have devised an *identification system* that is as simple as it is helpful: the portrayed birds are divided into five groups, each group of birds is given its own *colour-key* (see opposite page); colour photos and text are arranged opposite each other on a double page spread and given matching numbers on the appropriate background colour. Key-coloured thumb-marks, which are also clearly visible on the outside of the book, facilitate finding the appropriate bird groups.

As an additional aid to identification, *Collins Nature Guide to Birds* includes drawings of bird silhouettes, birds in flight, female and winter plumages, which are gathered together in picture keys. With their help, the inexperienced observer can learn how to tell similar species apart.

Over and above its purpose as an identification guide this book will inform you about how our birds live and create a feeling of responsibility for these creatures. Only those who feel responsible will support the protection of our bird life and therefore its conservation.

Colour key to groups of birds

Colour	Page numbers	Bird groups
	10–51	BLUE includes grebes and divers, shearwaters and petrels, gannet, cormorants, herons, spoonbill, storks, flamingo, wildfowl (swans, geese, ducks) – birds that live in and on the water
	52–83	PINK includes birds of prey, such as kites, hawks, buzzards, eagles, vultures, harriers and falcons, as well as owls
	84–141	YELLOW includes bustards, crakes and rails, crane, waders, skuas, gulls, terns, auks, sandgrouse – birds that mainly live on the shore, in marshes or on the steppes
	142–164	GREY includes nightjars, swifts, grouse, gamebirds, pigeons and doves, cuckoo, kingfisher, roller, bee-eater, hoopoe, wryneck and woodpeckers
	165–249	GREEN includes songbirds such as larks, swallows, pipits and wagtails, shrikes, warblers, flycatchers, thrushes, tits, wren, buntings, finches, sparrows, crows

This arrangement means that there are few exceptions to the normal systematic order.

How to start identifying birds

Place the bird you want to identify into one of the five key colours. With the help of the fieldmarks shown in the colour photos and described in the text you will be able to place your bird in its family and then find the species.

The choice of species

In this guide you will find almost all the bird species which breed in the roughly 10 million square kilometre region which stretches from the Atlantic coast in the west to the Urals in the east, from Greenland and Scandinavia in the north to the Mediterranean in the south. Only a few species breeding in Europe on the edge of their range or just occurring in small numbers are not treated.

PARTS OF THE BODY AND FEATHER TRACTS OF A BIRD
The diagram shows the important feather tracts and parts of a bird's body, together with a key.

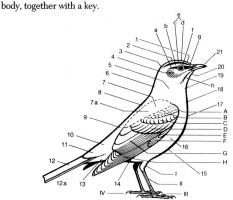

1	Forehead	14	Vent	H	Primaries
2	Crown	15	Belly	I	Thigh
3	Rear crown	16	Flanks/sides	II	Leg/tarsus
4	Cheeks (ear-coverts)	17	Breast	III	Toes and claws
5	Side of neck	18	Upper breast	IV	Hind toe
6	Nape	19	Throat	a	Eyestripe
7	Shoulder	20	Chin	b	Supercilium
7a	Scapulars	21	Bill	c	Lateral crown stripe
8	Upper back } Mantle	A	Bend of wing/carpal	d	Central crown stripe
9	Lower back }	B	Lesser (wing-)coverts	e	Crown
10	Rump	C	Median (wing-)coverts	f	Eyering
11	Upper tail-coverts	D	Greater (wing-)coverts	g	Loral stripe/lores
12	Tail	E	Alula	h	Malar stripe
12a	Outer tail feathers	F	Primary coverts		
13	Under tail-coverts	G	Tertials and secondaries		

Explanation

The COLOUR PHOTOGRAPHS are of wild birds; they portray the birds with their most important identification marks and in typical posture. As a rule the male in breeding plumage is shown. In many cases, when the two sexes are clearly different, colour photos of each sex are included. Birds which are to be found in northwest Europe mainly in non-breeding plumage are usually shown in this dress.

The DESCRIPTIONS of the pictured birds contain important details, which help with identification as a supplement to the colour photos — for example plumage marks, flight behaviour or song, by which the bird often first comes to attention. After the English name of the bird comes the scientific name, then in brackets that of the family.

Occurrence in Britain
The months in which the species is regularly found in Britain.

Identification
First the length of the adults in centimetres (from bill-tip to tail-tip) and the average weight in grams or kilograms are given. Where there is a significant difference in length or weight between the sexes, details are given separately for male and female. After that are given characteristic plumage and structural details as well as a description of any typical behaviour. The diagram on page 6 should help you to familiarise yourself with the topography of a bird.

Flight
Details are given for those species whose flight silhouette and behaviour is an important aid to identification.

Voice, song
The commonest calls and the song, normally given by the male in the breeding season, are decribed here.

Habitat
Description of the type of countryside in which the species breeds.

Food
Details of what the species eats.

Breeding
The breeding season of most European birds lasts at least two months. Most species only have a single brood in a year; a second brood may occur when the young of the first brood are reared to independence and the adults then start the cycle again. The clutch size given is the average; incubation period and fledging period are given in days, the age at which the young bird becomes independent or able to fly is given in weeks or days, as well as details of the siting and construction of the nest.

Similar species

Sometimes show only insignificant differences from the pictured species; differences in colour, size and habitat are given.

Drawings

Silhouettes are given of those species which can easily be confused with one another; with the help of these drawings, done specially for this guide, you can get a better idea of the typical jizz and posture of a particular bird and the relative sizes of different species. Flight pictures are also given of birds of prey, as well as female plumages of sea ducks and sawbills and winter plumages of grebes and divers. These drawings are arranged together in picture keys next to their appropriate colour key or on the end-papers.

The drawings in the text show the birds in characteristic posture or typical behaviour; they show important fieldmarks or the distinguishing marks of similar species.

Symbols and abbreviations at a glance

cm = size of the adult bird (from bill-tip to tail-tip) in centimetres
g/kg = weight of the adult bird in grams/kilograms

Distribution maps

Red areas represent the bird's **breeding range**. The area below the heavy dotted line, or enclosed by it, is the bird's **winter range**. This does not mean that the bird occurs everywhere within these limits, but locally where its proper habitat is available. If the bird's winter range is identical to its breeding range, or if the bird leaves the area entirely in winter there is no dotted line.

For more information

On the opposite page you will find addresses for further help. The species index (page 250) will enable you to look up those species whose names you know; it also includes the names of all bird families.

The authors

Professor Dr Jürgen Nicolai Director of the Institute for Bird Research in Wilhelmshaven, Professor of Zoology at the University of Hamburg.

Detlef Singer Biologist, freelance employee of the chair of landscape ecology in Weihenstephan, lecturer at the Munich adult education centre.

Konrad Wothe Biologist, nature photographer, film worker for the Institute for Scientific Film, for Heinz Sielmann and the ZDF.

Hermann Kacher Designer, animal illustrator, scientific illustrator at the Max-Planck-Institute Seewiesen.

Useful addresses
Ornithological societies and organisations

Royal Society for the Protection of Birds (RSPB)
The Lodge
Sandy
Bedfordshire
SG19 2DL
Europe's largest voluntary wildlife conservation body with over 850,000 members. Works for the conservation of wild birds and their habitats. Members receive *Birds* magazine four times a year; get free access to more than 100 reserves.

Young Ornithologists' Club (YOC)
The Lodge
Sandy
Bedfordshire
SG19 2DL
The junior branch of the RSPB. Members receive *Bird Life* six times a year.

British Trust for Ornithology (BTO)
National Centre for Ornithology
The Nunnery
Thetford
Norfolk
IP24 2PU
Coordinates bird surveys and monitoring by its members. Produces *Bird Study* and *BTO News*

British Ornithologists' Union
c/o Zoological Museum
Akeman Street
Tring
Herts
HP23 6AP
Publishes *The Ibis*

Wildfowl & Wetlands Trust
Slimbridge
Gloucester
GL2 7BT

Scottish Ornithologists' Club (SOC)
21 Regent Terrace
Edinburgh
EH7 5BT

Irish Wildbird Conservancy (IWC)
Ruttledge House
8 Longford Place
Monkstown
Co. Dublin

BirdLife International
Wellbrook Court
Girton Road
Cambridge
CB3 0NA

There are also local groups and societies. The RSPB has many local members' groups, and most counties have their own bird club or society. For more information on these, consult **The Birdwatcher's Yearbook & Diary**, published annually by Buckingham Press. All good libraries should have this invaluable reference source.

Bird magazines
Bird magazines, in addition to those produced by the above organisations for their members, include:

British Birds
Blunham, Bedford

Birding World
Cley-next-the-Sea, Norfolk

Birdwatch
London

Bird Watching
Peterborough

Great Crested Grebe

Podiceps cristatus

(Grebes)

In Britain: Jan-Dec.

Identification: 48 cm/1.1 kg. Largest European grebe; very long neck, slim head with long bill; unmistakable in breeding plumage with erectile feather 'ears' and chestnut, dark-edged 'side whiskers'; upperparts blackish-brown. In winter loses head and neck adornments, and appears much paler, with white extending above eye. Sexes similar. Young birds with striped head. Flight fast and direct with rapid wingbeats; in spring impressive courtship display, outside breeding season often in small groups.

Voice: A hoarse *'gruck gruck'*; in spring *'arr', 'k'pkk'p', 'ktik'*.

Habitat: Lakes, reservoirs and ponds with reedy fringes; in winter also on the coast.

Food: Small fish, insects, crustaceans.

Breeding: May-Jul, 3-5 eggs, incubation 27-29 days, young independent after 10-11 weeks. Floating nest.

breeding plumage

winter plumage

Red-necked Grebe

Podiceps grisegena

(Grebes)

In Britain: Sep-Apr.

Identification: 43 cm/750 g. Smaller and stockier than Great Crested Grebe, with shorter, thicker chestnut neck; cheeks and throat white; bill dark with yellow base. In winter plumage upperparts and neck dark grey, throat and cheeks pale showing distinct contrast, no pale stripe above eye. Sexes similar. When searching for food, usually in reed fringe or among water plants; often nests in Black-headed Gull colonies for protection.

Voice: Very vocal in spring, a whinnying *'oeerh'* repeated 5-10 times, a Mallard-like *'akakaakaak-aakak-aakak'*; when disturbed a short *'ek'*.

Habitat: Shallow lakes and ponds with a broad reed fringe, often with only a small area of open water.

Food: Aquatic insects and their larvae, frogs, snails, small fish.

Breeding: May-Jul, 4-5 eggs, incubation 22-25 days, young independent after 8-10 weeks. Floating nest.

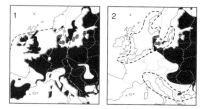

Black-necked Grebe

Podiceps nigricollis

(Grebes)

In Britain: Jan-Dec; rare breeder.
Identification: 30 cm/350 g. Upperparts, head and neck black, flanks chestnut, golden yellow fan of feathers on side of the head; gleaming red eyes; short, black, somewhat upturned bill. In winter plumage upperparts dark grey, underparts whitish. Sexes similar. Very sociable.
Voice: Piping, mournful *'huid'*; in spring repeated shivering *'vrib-bib'*.
Habitat: Thickly vegetated ponds and lakes.
Food: Insects, snails, tadpoles, crustaceans.
Breeding: May-Jul, 3-4 eggs, incubation 20-21 days, young independent after 5 weeks. Floating nest.

Little Grebe

Tachybaptus ruficollis

(Grebes)

In Britain: Jan-Dec.
Identification: 27 cm/200 g. Smallest European grebe, appears dumpy; short bill with pale tip, yellow patch at base; sides of head and neck chestnut-brown, top of head and neck dark brown (Plate 2). In winter plumage (Plate 3) unobtrusive grey brown, flanks paler. Sexes similar. Sociable in winter.
Voice: In spring long descending trill, often uttered by male and female in duet; when disturbed *'pit'*.
Habitat: Thickly vegetated ponds, lakes, rivers close to bank.
Food: Insects, small crustaceans, tadpoles.
Breeding: Apr-Jul, 4-6 eggs, incubation 19-21 days, young fledge at about 42 days; usually double-brooded. Floating nest.

Slavonian Grebe

Podiceps auritus

(Grebes)

In Britain: Jan-Dec; scarce breeder.
Identification: 31-38 cm/375 g. Chestnut neck contrasting with black head, orange-yellow tuft of feathers straight back from eye ('horns'); brownish-black upperparts, chestnut flanks. Sexes similar. In winter black and white, cleaner-looking than Black-necked Grebe, with straight bill.
Voice: Low rippling trill; harsh nasal notes.
Habitat: Clear northern lakes with dense fringing vegetation. In winter coastal waters, estuaries.
Food: Insects, crustaceans, small fish.
Breeding: May-Aug, 4-5 eggs, incubation 22-25 days, young fledge at 55-60 days. Floating nest.

1 Red-throated Diver

Gavia stellata

(Divers)

In Britain: Jan-Dec.

Identification: 53-58 cm/1-2 kg. Not much bigger than Great Crested Grebe (p. 10); bill upturned; back dark, unpatterned; head and sides of neck ash-grey; in breeding plumage red stripe down front of neck; eyes red. In winter plumage similar to Black-throated Diver, but rather paler, back with small white spots. Sexes similar. Swims with head held angled upwards.

Voice: Harsh *'gre-gre-gre'*; in breeding season *'okok-ker'*, *'miao'*, *'auua'*; in flight *'gak gak'*. *Habitat:* Lakes, also tundra pools. *Food:* Fish, crustaceans, frogs. *Breeding:* May-Jul, 2 eggs, incubation 24-29 days, young fledge at 6 weeks. Nests on bank.

2 Great Northern Diver

Gavia immer

(Divers)

In Britain: Oct-May.

Identification: 70-90 cm/4 kg. Our largest diver, with stout neck and heavy bill, 'bump' on forehead; black head and neck with partial white collar, upperparts black, chequered white, white underparts. Sexes similar. In winter dark grey-brown and white, head and neck darker than back (the opposite of Black-throated Diver).

Voice: Vocal when breeding, a far-carrying, desolate musical wailing *'aaooooah'*. Otherwise silent.

Habitat: Undisturbed northern forest lakes; in winter in coastal waters. *Food:* Mainly fish, also crustaceans, molluscs.

Breeding: Jun-Jul, 2 eggs, incubation 24-25 days, young fledge at 70-77 days. Nests on bank or island.

3 Black-throated Diver

Gavia arctica

(Divers)

In Britain: Jan-Dec.

Identification: 58-68 cm/2-3 kg. Larger and stockier than Great Crested Grebe (p. 10); head and hind-neck grey, appearing inflated; back black with white chequering. In winter plumage upperparts uniform dark grey-brown. Sexes similar. Usually swims with head held horizontally; dives up to 3 minutes long.

Voice: In spring rising, wailing *'a-uuua, auuqui auuihuuih'*; far-carrying barking *'vau-a'*. *Habitat:* Large, unpolluted lakes. *Food:* Fish.

Breeding: May-Jul, 2 eggs, incubation 28-30 days, young fledge at 2 months. Nests on bank or island.

1

2

3

1   Storm Petrel   *Hydrobates pelagicus*

(Storm-petrels)

In Britain: Apr-Oct.

Identification: 14-18 cm/25 g. Small sooty-black seabird with obvious white rump, also short white bar on underwing; superficially resembles House Martin (p. 170).

Flight: Low over sea, erratic; sometimes follows boats.

Voice: Churring and clucking notes by night on breeding grounds; *'arrrr-r-r'*, with terminal *'chick-a'*.

Habitat: Pelagic; only comes ashore by night to breed.

Food: Plankton, floating offal, small fish.

Breeding: Jun-Jul, 1 egg, incubation 38-43 days, young fledge at 59-75 days. Nests in burrow, crevice in rocks or walls.

2   Manx Shearwater   *Puffinus puffinus*

(Shearwaters and petrels)

In Britain: Feb-Oct.

Identification: 35 cm/440 g. Near Black-headed Gull in size; black bill; sharp contrast between black head and upperparts and white underparts. The upperparts of the Mediterranean Shearwater (until recently regarded as a race of Manx) are brown, the underparts greyish-white. Sexes similar.

Flight: Stocky body, very narrow wings; underwing coverts white. Glides on stiff wings low over the waves.

Voice: Loud crowing and squawking calls at breeding site.

Habitat: Open sea; breeds on rocky coasts.

Food: Fish, crustaceans, invertebrates, carrion, offal.

Breeding: May-Sep, 1 egg, incubation 52-54 days, young fledge at 72-73 days. Colonial nester, each pair in own burrow.

3   Fulmar   *Fulmarus glacialis*

(Shearwaters and petrels)

In Britain: Jan-Dec.

Identification: 48 cm/750 g. Superficially resembles Herring Gull (p. 130), but head and neck thicker; short bill with 'tubes' on top; mainly white with silver grey upperparts, pale grey rump and tail. Sexes similar. Regularly follows ships.

Flight: Flies in long arcs on stiff wings close to the sea surface.

Voice: Cackling and grunting noises. *Habitat:* Open sea; breeds on steep cliffs.

Food: Dead fish, jellyfish, corpses of sea mammals.

Breeding: May-Sep, 1 egg, incubation 55-57 days, young fledge at 46-51 days. Colonial nester on cliff ledges.

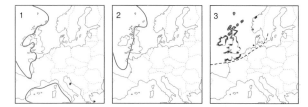

1 Gannet

Sula bassana

(Gannets)

In Britain: Jan-Dec.
Identification: 91 cm/3 kg. Goose-sized, white seabird with black primaries and powerful, long pointed beak; head and neck creamy yellow. Sexes similar. Young dark brown with finely spotted upperparts. When fishing plunges into sea from height of up to 40 m.
Flight: Cigar-shaped body, long wings with black tips, long wedge-shaped tail.
Voice: On breeding site rough, throaty *'kirra kirra'*; barking *'arreh'*, hard *'arr'*.
Habitat: Sea, usually coastal waters. *Food:* Fish.
Breeding: Apr-Aug. 1 egg, incubation 43-45 days, young fledge at 90 days. Colonial nester on steep cliffs, rocky islands.

2 Shag

Phalacrocorax aristotelis

(Cormorants)

In Britain: Jan-Dec.
Identification: 76 cm/1850 g. Smaller than Cormorant. Neck thinner and shorter; bill black with yellow gape; plumage black with greenish gloss; in breeding plumage has forward-curved crest. Sexes similar. Young birds brown without gloss. Leaps clear of water when diving for fish.
Flight: Like Cormorant, but wing beats more rapid.
Voice: Rasping *'k-arr'*, *'arck arck'*, *'kroack-kraik-kroack'*.
Habitat: Coastal waters, rocky coasts when breeding.
Food: Mainly herrings, sandeels.
Breeding: Mar-Jul, 3-5 eggs, incubation 30 days, young fledge at 55 days. Colonial nester on cliffs.

3 Cormorant

Phalacrocorax carbo

(Cormorants)

In Britain: Jan-Dec.
Identification: 90 cm/2.5 kg. Large, black waterbird with white cheeks and chin; large bill, hooked at tip; plumage glistening bronze; in breeding plumage white patch on thigh. Sexes similar. Young brown above. Swims low in water, head and bill held angled upwards.
Flight: Long narrow wings, outstretched neck and long wedge-shaped tail.
Voice: At breeding site *'khro khro'*, *'krao'*.
Habitat: Large lakes, sea coasts. *Food:* Fish.
Breeding: Apr-Jul, 3-5 eggs, incubation 23-29 days, young fledge at 47-50 days. Colonial nester in trees and on rocks.

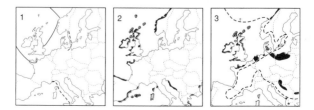

1 White Pelican
Pelecanus onocrotalus

(Pelicans)

In Britain: Not recorded.
Identification: 140-180 cm/10-11 kg. Very large, white waterbird; neck and bill long, with elastic yellow throat pouch; when breeding, plumage with pink flush. Female smaller than male. Young brown, becoming dirty white. Soars often for long periods, very high and in formation.
Flight: Long, broad wings with black tips and broad, black trailing edge.
Voice: When breeding groaning and grunting noises.
Habitat: Extensive marshes, river deltas. *Food:* Fish.
Breeding: May-Jul, 1-3 eggs, incubation 29-30 days, young leave nest at 20-30 days, independent at 65-70 days. Colonial nester.

2 Purple Heron
Ardea purpurea

(Herons)

In Britain: Rare visitor, mainly Apr-May.
Identification: 79 cm/950 g. Smaller, more slender and darker than Grey Heron; neck very thin, chestnut-brown with broad black longitudinal stripes; whitish and rusty-red ornamental plumes hanging from back. Sexes similar. Remains mostly hidden in reedbeds.
Flight: Quicker wingbeats than Grey Heron, appears darker.
Voice: Normally silent; flight call 'kreck'.
Habitat: Extensive marshy areas with dense reedbeds.
Food: Small fish, frogs, small mammals, insects.
Breeding: Apr-Jun, 4-5 eggs, incubation 25-28 days, young fledge at 45-50 days. Colonial nester.

3 Grey Heron
Ardea cinerea

(Herons)

In Britain: Jan-Dec.
Identification: 91 cm/ 1.6 kg. Almost stork-sized, mainly grey; bill yellowish, in spring orange; black stripe over eye; long thin black plumes from back of head. Sexes similar. Young washed-out grey. Seeks food on banks of shallow waters, in meadows and fields.
Flight: Slow, deep wingbeats, neck held retracted in 'S'; does not glide like storks.
Voice: Hoarse croaking 'kraak' or 'khroe'; in flight often 'kreik'.
Habitat: Waterside, wet meadows.
Food: Fish, amphibians, worms, small mammals, insects.
Breeding: Mar-Jun, 3-5 eggs, incubation 25-28 days, young fledge at 50-55 days. Colonial nester; nest of sticks in tall trees, occasionally in reedbeds.

1 Cattle Egret

Bubulcus ibis

(Herons)

In Britain: Rare visitor.

Identification: 51 cm/350 g. Small white heron, stockier than Little Egret; bill short, yellow; when breeding, rich buff plumes on top of head, back and breast, reddish legs (Plate shows non-breeding plumage). Often among cattle, catches insects disturbed by them; rides on large animals searching for skin parasites.

Voice: When breeding crow-like croaking.

Habitat: Marshy areas, meadows; not so dependent on water as other herons.

Food: Large insects (especially grasshoppers, dragonflies), water beetles, snails, frogs.

Breeding: Apr-Jun, 4-5 eggs, incubation 21-25 days, young fledge at 30 days. Colonial nester; nests in bushes and trees.

2 Little Egret

Egretta garzetta

(Herons)

In Britain: Jan-Dec; scarce visitor, increasing.

Identification: 56 cm/500 g. Small white heron; bill and legs black, feet yellow; in breeding plumage long ornamental plumes on back of head, breast and back. Sexes similar. Feeds in shallow water, sometimes also among grazing cattle.

Voice: When breeding croaking and rasping sounds.

Habitat: Marshland with trees and bushes, thickly vegetated banks of large rivers; rice paddies.

Food: Small fish, frogs, crustaceans, aquatic insects.

Breeding: May-Jul, 3-5 eggs, incubation 21-25 days, young fledge at 30 days. Colonial nester; nests in trees or bushes.

3 Great White Egret

Egretta alba

(Herons)

In Britain: Rare vagrant.

Identification: 89 cm/1.5 kg. Grey Heron-sized, slender, snow-white heron; in breeding plumage ornamental plumes hang from back over wings; neck very long and thin; when breeding, bill black with yellow base, otherwise yellow (Plate). Legs and feet greenish-black. Sexes similar. When feeding wades slowly through water.

Voice: When breeding a croaking *'rhe'* or *'rha'*.

Habitat: Large reedbeds by water. *Food:* Fish, amphibians, aquatic insects.

Breeding: Apr-Jun, 3-4 eggs, incubation 25-26 days, young fledge at 40-44 days. Colonial nester; nests in reeds or bushes.

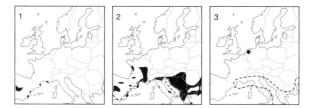

Squacco Heron

Ardeola ralloides

(Herons)

In Britain: Rare vagrant.
Identification: 46 cm/280 g. Small stocky heron with thick neck; plumage rich golden-buff; underparts, wings and tail white; elongated feathers on head, striped dark, hang down to shoulders; legs yellowish-green. In winter-dress head and neck finely streaked dark. Sexes similar. Young striped grey-brown on head, neck, breast and back. Mainly crepuscular; prefers cover, often in thick bushes on marshes; occasionally stands upright in reeds like Bittern.
Flight: Appears suddenly white.
Voice: When breeding a hoarse 'karrr' or 'kerrr'; squawking.
Habitat: Extensive lowland marshes with scattered bushes, shallow lakes, river deltas. _Food:_ Aquatic insects, leeches, crustaceans, tadpoles, small fish.
Breeding: May-Jul, 4-6 eggs, incubation 22-24 days, young fledge at 45 days. Colonial nester; nests in bushes and trees, in reedbeds.

Night Heron

Nycticorax nycticorax

(Herons)

In Britain: Rare visitor.
Identification: 61 cm/550 g. Small, stocky, short-necked heron; crown and back blue-black, wings grey, underparts dirty white; long white thread-like plumes on nape; bill relatively short, black; eyes ruby-red. Sexes similar. Young dark brown, upperparts spotted white. Chiefly active at dusk and by night, by day rests hidden in trees; seeks food in damp meadows and ditches.
Flight: Relatively short, rounded wings; flies silently like owl with deep wingbeats.
Voice: When disturbed and in flight 'ark' or 'quok'; when breeding hoarse croaking.
Habitat: Extensive marshlands with groups of trees and bushes; rivers with quiet backwaters and undisturbed vegetation.
Food: Small fish, frogs, tadpoles, aquatic insects, leeches, small mammals.
Breeding: Apr-Jun, 3-4 eggs, incubation 21 days, young fledge at 40-44 days. Colonial nester; nests in osiers, trees, or reedbeds.

young   adult

Bittern

1

Botaurus stellaris

(Herons)

In Britain: Jan-Dec; scarce.

Identification: 76 cm/1.2 kg. Large stocky heron with thick neck; plumage mainly yellow-brown (reed-coloured), banded and striped darker; crown black, throat white. Sexes similar. Steals slowly through reeds; when threatened freezes with head and bill pointing vertically ('Bittern-stance').

Flight: Broad rounded wings, neck drawn back.

Voice: Recalling distant foghorn, muffled *'iu-vump'*; in flight *'ahrk'*.

Habitat: Extensive reedbeds. *Food:* Fish, amphibians, leeches, aquatic insects.

Breeding: Mar-May, 3-6 eggs, incubation 25-26 days, young fledge at 14-20 days. Flat nest in reeds.

Little Bittern

2

Ixobrychus minutus

(Herons)

In Britain: Apr-Sep; rare visitor, has bred.

Identification: 35 cm/140 g. Very small heron with thick neck and long, green toes; crown, back and wings greenish-black, wing-coverts creamy-buff, underparts yellowish; female straw-coloured, upperparts spotted brown, underparts striped. When threatened often adopts 'Bittern-stance' for several minutes; crepuscular.

Voice: Display call recalling distant barking dog *'vu'* or *'vug'*; flight call *'ker'*.

Habitat: Shallow water-bodies with thick reedbeds.

Food: Small fish, frogs, tadpoles, aquatic insects.

Breeding: May-Jul, 5-6 eggs, incubation 16-19 days, young fledge at 25-30 days. Shallow cup-shaped nest in reeds.

Spoonbill

3

Platalea leucorodia

(Ibises and spoonbills)

In Britain: Jan-Dec; scarce visitor, does not breed.

Identification: 86 cm/2 kg. Grey Heron-sized, all white; long black spoon-shaped bill with yellow tip; yellow patch on breast; in breeding plumage yellowish tuft of feathers on nape. Sexes similar. When feeding sweeps bill from side to side through water; flies in formation. In flight neck outstretched, somewhat drooping.

Voice: When breeding grunting noises.

Habitat: Extensive wetlands with shallow water-bodies and reedbeds.

Food: Small fish, mussels, snails, tadpoles, aquatic insects.

Breeding: Apr-Jul, 3-5 eggs, incubation 21-25 days, young fledge at 45-50 days. Colonial breeder; nest usually in reeds.

1 White Stork
(Storks) *Ciconia ciconia*

In Britain: Rare visitor.
Identification: 102 cm/3.4 kg. Large white wading bird with black flight feathers, long red bill and long bright red legs. Sexes similar. Young birds with brownish bill. Soars for long periods, often at a great height; when searching for food walks majestically.
Flight: Outstretched neck, legs extending well beyond tail.
Voice: Bill-clappering (greeting).
Habitat: Wetlands, meadows, river valleys with clumps of trees.
Food: Frogs, mice, insects, earthworms.
Breeding: Mar-Jun, 3-5 eggs, incubation 31-34 days, young fledge at 58-64 days. Large stick nest on buildings, in trees.

2 Black Stork
(Storks) *Ciconia nigra*

In Britain: Rare vagrant.
Identification: 97 cm/3 kg. Mainly black with metallic green and purple gloss; belly and undertail coverts white; bill and legs red. Sexes similar. Often soars at great height for hours on thermals; very shy.
Flight: Neck and wings black, belly and 'armpits' white; neck outstretched.
Voice: Flight call *'fiio'*; when disturbed *'fiehhh'*.
Habitat: Ancient deciduous and evergreen forests with streams, ponds, natural water-bodies. *Food:* Fish, newts, frogs.
Breeding: Apr-Jul, 3-5 eggs, incubation 32-35 days, young fledge at 62-69 days. Large stick nest in trees.

3 Greater Flamingo
(Flamingos) *Phoenicopterus ruber*

In Britain: Not recorded.
Identification: 127 cm/male 3.5 kg, female 2.5 kg. Large, very slender; neck and legs out of proportion; pinkish-white with crimson in the wing; pink bill, bent down in the middle, bill tip black. Often in dense flocks.
Flight: Wing-coverts scarlet-red, black flight feathers; flocks fly in V-formation or in irregular chains.
Voice: Goose-like *'kakak'* or *'gragra'*, also guttural trumpeting sound.
Habitat: Shallow saline or brackish lakes, coastal lagoons.
Food: Small crustaceans, aquatic insects, insect larvae, worms, invertebrates.
Breeding: Apr-Jul, 1 egg, incubation 28-32 days, young leave nest after 10 days, fledge at 70-75 days. Colonial breeder; bowl-shaped nest on ground.

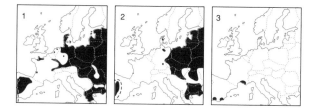

1   Mute Swan

Cygnus olor

(Wildfowl)

In Britain: Jan-Dec.

Identification: 152 cm/10-22 kg. Pure white with orange-red bill with black basal knob. Occurs semi-tame on park lakes. Sexes similar.

Voice: Almost completely silent, only occasionally a hoarse hissing in defence.

Habitat: Inland lakes and pools with shallow, well vegetated margins and large areas of open water. *Food:* Chiefly submerged plants.

Breeding: Apr-Jul, 5-7 eggs, incubation 34-38 days, young fledge at 4 to 5 months. Nests on ground.

2   Whooper Swan

Cygnus cygnus

(Wildfowl)

In Britain: Oct-Apr; winter visitor.

Identification: 152 cm/7-12 kg. Like Mute Swan, but bill black with extensive yellow base, no bill-knob, neck longer and carried erect. Lacks obvious wing noise in flight. Sexes similar.

Voice: Noisy; when swimming a goose-like *'ang'*, in flight a disyllabic *'ang ha'*.

Habitat: Northern tundra and taiga; in winter regular on lakes and coasts.

Food: Submerged vegetation, young cereals, grass.

Breeding: May-Jul, 3-6 eggs, incubation 35-42 days, young fledge at 3 months. Nests on ground.

Mute Swan

Whooper Swan

Bewick's Swan

3   Bewick's Swan

Cygnus columbianus

(Wildfowl)

In Britain: Nov-Mar; winter visitor.

Identification: 122 cm/5-7 kg. Very similar to Whooper Swan, but smaller, neck shorter, yellow on bill less extensive, not extending to a point.

Voice: Call higher and softer than Whooper Swan, *'huh huh'* or *'kuru'*.

Habitat: Tundra north of the tree line and taiga; in winter on freshwater lakes and flooded meadows. *Food:* Aquatic plants, grass, young cereals.

Breeding: Jun-Jul, 3-5 eggs, incubation 29-30 days, young fledge at 8 weeks or less. Nests on ground.

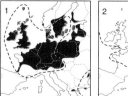

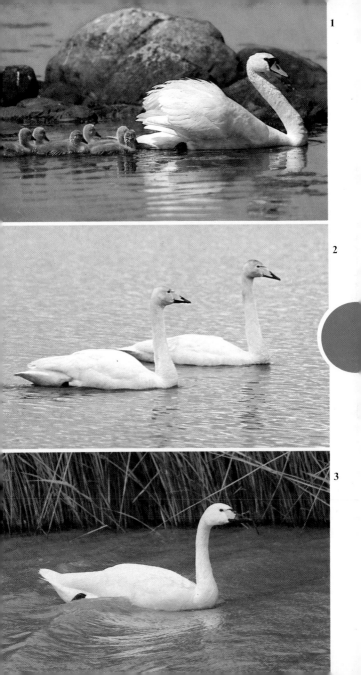

1 Greylag Goose
Anser anser

(Wildfowl)

In Britain: Jan-Dec; the introduced population is resident.

Identification: 76-89 cm/2.3-4 kg. Silvery grey plumage, bill pinkish to orange, feet flesh-coloured. Domestic geese derive from this species. In pairs in breeding season, otherwise in family parties or larger flocks.

Voice: Similar to farmyard goose, though less loud and insistent, more sparing in uttering loud noises; call in flight a drawling *'aahng-ong-ong'*; contact call *'gagaga'*.

Habitat: Large lakes with dense fringing vegetation (reeds, rushes), bordered by meadows and pasture, extensive marshy areas. Also gravel pits.

Food: Entirely vegetable matter; grass, young cereals, leaves and young shoots of clover, dandelions. Feeds on land, not in water.

Breeding: Apr-Jul, 5-6 eggs, incubation 28-29 days, young fledge at 8 weeks. Nests on ground.

2 Pink-footed Goose
Anser brachyrhynchus

(Wildfowl)

In Britain: Sep-May.

Identification: 60-75 cm/2.5 kg. Smaller than Greylag Goose. Blue-grey upperparts, pale brown underparts; head and neck contrasting darker; short pink bill with black markings; pink legs. In flight pale blue-grey forewing.

Voice: Rather high disyllabic *'wink-wink'*, *'unk-unk'*.

Habitat: Tundra, low cliffs; in winter farmland, estuaries.

Food: Grain, root vegetables, grass.

Breeding: May-Jun, 3-6 eggs, incubation 26-27 days, young fledge at 56 days. Nests on ground.

3 Bean Goose
Anser fabalis

(Wildfowl)

In Britain: Nov-Mar; uncommon winter visitor.

Identification: 71-89 cm/3-4 kg. Size of Greylag, plumage much browner in tone (not grey), and much darker on head, neck and back; head and bill longer; bill black with orange band; legs orange-yellow.

Voice: Not as vocal as Greylag; call in flight a hurried *'kayak kayak'* or a deep bugling *'ang ang'*.

Habitat: Lakes in lightly wooded taiga; in winter fields, pastures and extensive wet grassland.

Food: Like Greylag; grass, young cereals, root crops.

Breeding: May-Jul, 4-6 eggs, incubation 27-29 days, young fledge at 8 weeks. Nests on ground.

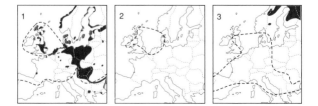

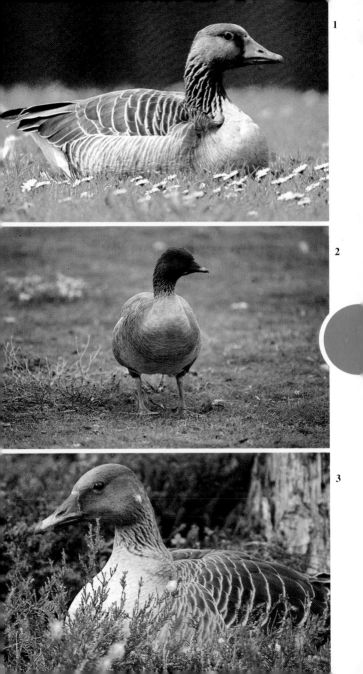

1

2

3

1 White-fronted Goose

Anser albifrons

(Wildfowl)

In Britain: Oct-Apr; migrant and winter visitor.
Identification: 68-76 cm/1.4-3.3 kg. Smaller than Greylag and Bean Geese (p. 32); white forehead (which gives it its name), irregular black barring on belly; bill pale pink (orange-yellow in Greenland race); legs orange.
Voice: Far-carrying, high-pitched 2- or 3-syllable call *'klii-klii'* or *'klik-klik-klik'*.
Habitat: Northern tundra; in winter coastal pastures, meadows.
Food: Grass and grass seed; in winter also saltmarsh vegetation.
Breeding: Jun-Jul, 5-6 eggs, incubation 27-28 days, young fledge at 6 weeks. Nests on ground.

2 Lesser White-fronted Goose

Anser erythropus

(Wildfowl)

In Britain: Rare winter visitor.
Identification: 53-68 cm/1.4-2 kg. Very similar to White-front, but smaller, shorter-necked and shorter-billed; narrow, bright yellow eye-ring.

Voice: Higher-pitched than White-front, very rapid *'kyu-lit kyu-lit'* or *'klick-klu-klick-klu'*.
Habitat: Northern taiga up into the edge of the tundra.
Food: Leaves and shoots of Dwarf Willow (*Salix herbacea*), grass.
Breeding: Jun-Jul, 4-5 eggs, incubation 25-28 days, young fledge at 5-6 weeks. Nests on ground.

3 Canada Goose

Branta canadensis

(Wildfowl)

In Britain: Jan-Dec; introduced.
Identification: 92-102 cm/3.6-5.4 kg. Very big, long-necked goose; head and neck black, cheeks and throat white. Sexes similar.
Voice: Far-carrying, trumpeting *'ah-honk'*, the most musical of the geese.
Habitat: Freshwater lakes and ponds, gravel pits, parks.
Food: Grass and vegetables, aquatic vegetation.
Breeding: Mar-Jun, 5-6 eggs, incubation 28-30 days, young fledge at 6-7 weeks. Nests on ground.

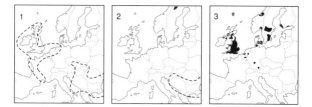

1 Barnacle Goose

Branta leucopsis

(Wildfowl)

In Britain: Oct-Apr; winter visitor to coastal areas.
Identification: 58-69 cm/1.4-2.4 kg. Smaller than White-fronted Goose (p. 34), conspicuous black-and-white head pattern visible at a great distance; back blue-grey, underparts whitish. Sexes similar.
Voice: Hoarse, polysyllabic call *'grigrigri'*, recalling distant barking of dogs.
Habitat: Northern tundra; in winter on mudflats and intertidal marshes.
Food: Grass; shoots and catkins of tundra willows; in winter also clover, seeds.
Breeding: Jun-Jul, 3-5 eggs, incubation 24-25 days, young fledge at 6-7 weeks. Nests on cliff ledge.

2 Brent Goose

Branta bernicla

(Wildfowl)

In Britain: Sep-Apr; winter visitor to North Sea and Channel coasts, Ireland.
Identification: 56-61 cm/1.1-1.7 kg. Smallest European goose; very dark, with white mark on side of neck, white 'stern'. The (Russian) birds wintering on the North Sea and Channel coasts have a dark belly.
Voice: Far-carrying *'rrott-rrott-rrott'*.
Habitat: Arctic tundra; in winter mudflats with eelgrass and green algae.
Food: Grass, moss, lichens; in winter eelgrass and green algae.
Breeding: Jun-Jul, 3-5 eggs, incubation 24-26 days. Nests on ground.

3 Shelduck

Tadorna tadorna

(Wildfowl)

In Britain: Jan-Dec.
Identification: 61 cm/800-1400 g. Conspicuous black, white and red plumage; bill coral-red, that of male with basal knob in breeding season. Female similar to male, though duller, bill without knob.
Voice: Very vocal; male a high piping *'huiiih'*; female a hard, rapid *'ak ak ak'*.
Habitat: Sea coasts, also inland waters.
Food: Cockles, snails, worms and small crustaceans.

female in flight

Breeding: Apr-Jul, 8-12 eggs, incubation 28-30 days, young fledge at 7-8 weeks. Nests in burrow.

1

2

3

1 Mallard

Anas platyrhynchos

(Wildfowl)

In Britain: Jan-Dec.

Identification: 58 cm/900-1500 g. Commonest European duck; male with bottle green head, white neck-ring, brown breast and pearl-grey upper- and underparts; female inconspicuous, brown; young like female.

Voice: Male hoarse *'riib riib';* female loud *'ahk ahk ahk'.*

Habitat: Shallow, standing waters, park lakes.

Food: Aquatic plants and animals, grain.

Breeding: Mar-Jul, 8-12 eggs, incubation 26-29 days, young fledge at 7-8 weeks. Nests on ground, also in willow pollards, on flat roofs.

Duckling

2 Gadwall

Anas strepera

(Wildfowl)

In Britain: Jan-Dec.

Identification: 51 cm/600-1300 g. Rather smaller than Mallard, more slender; male mainly grey, wing-coverts brown, 'stern' black, speculum white; female similar to female Mallard but bill orange-yellow, speculum white; young like female.

Voice: Male deep nasal *'tuh tuh';* female quacking *'reck reck reck'.*

Habitat: Standing or slowly flowing waters with rich fringing vegetation.

Food: Aquatic plants and seeds, small animals.

Breeding: May-Jul, 8-12 eggs, incubation 25-27 days, young fledge at 7 weeks. Nests on ground.

3 Pintail

Anas acuta

(Wildfowl)

In Britain: Jan-Dec; rare breeder.

Identification: 66 cm/600-1100 g. Slimmer than Mallard with long thin neck and long pointed tail; male head and upper neck dark brown, long white stripe up side of neck; female grey-brown.

Voice: In courtship male utters a *'kriuck'* or piping *'pfiub';* female rasping quack.

Habitat: Northern tundra, bogs, marshes.

Food: Chiefly aquatic plants, also aquatic animals.

Breeding: Apr-Jun, 7-11 eggs, incubation 21-23 days, otherwise as Gadwall.

1

2

3

1

Teal

Anas crecca

(Wildfowl)

In Britain: Jan-Dec.

Identification: 36 cm/250-350 g. Smallest European duck; male head bright chestnut with broad green band on side; female mottled brown. Very sociable.

Voice: In courtship male utters high, piping *'kriuck'*; female a rapid *'gegege'*.

Habitat: Standing or slowly flowing waters, moorland.

Food: In summer mainly insect larvae, molluscs, in winter aquatic plants, seeds.

Breeding: Apr-Jun, 8-10 eggs, incubation 21-25 days, young fledge at 4 weeks. Nests on ground.

2

Garganey

Anas querquedula

(Wildfowl)

In Britain: Mar-Sep.

Identification: 38 cm/300-450 g. A little larger than Teal; male head, neck and breast brown, with striking white stripe over eye, forewing blue-grey, belly white; female like female Teal, but with more contrasting head pattern and longer bill.

Voice: In courtship male utters a grating mechanical *'klerr-reb'*; female call similar to Mallard but higher-pitched *'kniik'*.

Habitat: Standing or slowly flowing inland waters with luxuriant plant growth.

Food: Like Teal.

Breeding: May-Jun, 8-11 eggs, incubation 23 days, young fledge at 5-6 weeks. Nests on ground.

3

Wigeon

Anas penelope

(Wildfowl)

In Britain: Jan-Dec; scarce breeder.

Identification: 46 cm/450-850 g. Smaller and more slender than Mallard (p. 38); male chestnut head, pale yellow forehead, white forewing, body pearl grey; female reddish-brown; young like female.

Voice: Male a whistling *'huituh'*; female a grating *'terrr'*.

Habitat: Northern tundra, bogs, in winter numerous on estuaries.

Food: Mainly marsh and aquatic plants, grazes like goose.

Breeding: May-Jun, 7-10 eggs, incubation 22-25 days, young fledge at 6 weeks. Nests on ground.

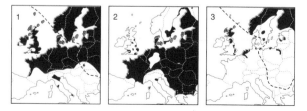

1 Shoveler

Anas clypeata

(Wildfowl)

In Britain: Jan-Dec.

Identification: 51 cm/500-800 g. Bill long and flared at tip like a shovel; male head glossed green, belly and flanks chestnut, breast white, forewing blue; female brownish like Mallard (p. 38), but bluish forewing.

Voice: Male a deep and hoarse *'tuk-tuk'*; female Mallard-like *'voak-voak'*.

Habitat: Shallow inland waters with rich vegetation.

Food: Sieves fine particles of food (seeds, small animals) from shallow water.

Breeding: May-Jun, 8-12 eggs, incubation 23-25 days, young fledge at 6-7 weeks. Nests on ground.

2 Red-crested Pochard

Netta rufina

(Wildfowl)

In Britain: Rare visitor; also escape from wildfowl collections.

Identification: 56 cm/800-1200 g. Male foxy-red head, with high forehead and rounded crown, breast black, upperparts brown, shoulders and flanks white, bill carmine-red; female grey-brown with pale cheeks.

Voice: Male a hoarse *'biit'*; female a grating *'kurr'*.

Habitat: Shallow, warm lakes and pools with thick fringing vegetation and large areas of open water.

Food: Mainly plant material, green algae.

Breeding: May-Jun, 6-12 eggs, incubation 26-28 days, young fledge at 6-7 weeks. Nests on ground.

3 Pochard

Aythya ferina

(Wildfowl)

In Britain: Jan-Dec.

Identification: 46 cm/600-1100 g. Somewhat larger than Tufted Duck (p. 44), stocky, big-headed; male head and neck chestnut-brown, breast and tail black, body pale grey; female grey-brown.

Voice: In courtship male utters a soft drawn-out whistling; female a croaking *'kharr-kharr'*.

Habitat: Large freshwater bodies with rich fringing vegetation, brackish lakes.

Food: Mainly aquatic plants.

Breeding: May-Jun, 8-11 eggs, incubation 24-26 days, young fledge at 7-8 weeks. Nests on ground.

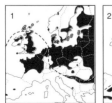

1

2

3

1 Tufted Duck

Aythya fuligula

(Wildfowl)

In Britain: Jan-Dec.

Identification: 43 cm/600-1000 g. Small stocky diving duck; male jet-black, flanks and belly white, head with purple gloss, long head tuft, eyes yellow; female uniform brown with short tuft, often with a narrow white band on forehead around the base of the bill.

Voice: In courtship male utters a soft whistling *'giu giu'*; female a rasping *'karr-karr'*.

Habitat: Standing or slowly flowing waters with vegetated banks and open water.

Food: Predominantly animal matter (molluscs, insect larvae).

Breeding: May-Aug, 8-10 eggs, incubation 23-25 days, young fledge at 7 weeks. Nests on ground.

2 Scaup

Aythya marila

(Wildfowl)

In Britain: Oct-Apr.

Identification: 48 cm/700-1300 g. A little larger than Tufted Duck; male black head with green gloss, neck, breast and tail matt black, back pale grey, underparts white, eyes yellow; female like Tufted Duck female, but white around base of bill more extensive.

Voice: In courtship male utters a soft cooing; female a deep *'karr-karr'*.

Habitat: Lakes and pools on the tundra and taiga; in winter on the sea.

Food: Molluscs, worms.

Breeding: May-Jul, 6-9 eggs, incubation 24-28 days, young fledge at 6 weeks. Nests on ground.

3 Ferruginous Duck

Aythya nyroca

(Wildfowl)

In Britain: Oct-Mar; rare visitor.

Identification: 41 cm/450-650 g. Small diving duck with the jizz of a dabbling duck, less compact than Tufted Duck and Pochard (p. 42). Male rich mahogany, undertail coverts gleaming white, eyes white; female dark brown with rufous tones, eyes dark.

Voice: Male a grating *'krrr-krrr-krrr'*; female a higher pitched *'gerr gerr'*.

Habitat: Standing inland waters with rich plant growth, small wooded lakes.

Food: Aquatic plants, including green algae.

Breeding: May-Jun, 8-10 eggs, incubation 25-27 days, young fledge at 8 weeks. Nests on ground.

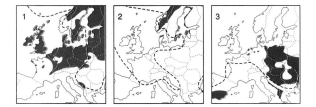

Eider

Somateria mollissima

(Wildfowl)

In Britain: Jan-Dec.

Identification: 58 cm/1.3-2.8 kg. Almost goose-sized, heavy seaduck with characteristic head profile; male upperparts white, underparts black, back of head and sides of neck pale green, top of head black; female (Plate 2) coloured like female Mallard (p. 38), but breast barred, easy to identify by general bulk and long head profile.

Voice: Male a musical *'uhuu-uhuu'*; female a deep *'korr korr'*.

Habitat: Sea coasts.

Food: Mussels, crabs, starfish.

Breeding: May-Jul, 4-6 eggs, incubation 25-26 days, young fledge at 9-10 weeks. Nests on ground.

Velvet Scoter

Melanitta fusca

(Wildfowl)

In Britain: Oct-May.

Identification: 56 cm/1.1-1.9 kg. Larger than Common Scoter; male pure black apart from white patch in wing and white mark under eye, bill orange-yellow, feet red; female blackish-brown with two pale areas on side of head.

Voice: Male *'kyu'* or *'kyuorr'*; female a vibrating *'braaa braaa'*.

Habitat: Male breeding, on taiga and tundra pools; in winter on the sea.

Food: Almost entirely molluscs, especially mussels.

Breeding: May-Jul, 7-10 eggs, incubation 27 days, young fledge at 7 weeks. Nests on ground.

Common Scoter

Melanitta nigra

(Wildfowl)

In Britain: Jan-Dec; rare breeder.

Identification: 48 cm/700-1400 g. The only entirely black duck (male), bill with orange patch; female dark brown with conspicuous pale cheeks. Told from the larger Velvet Scoter by complete lack of white in plumage.

Voice: Male piping and cooing; female grating call.

Habitat: When breeding, on taiga and tundra lakes and pools; in autumn and winter on the sea.

Food: Almost entirely molluscs, especially mussels.

Breeding: Jun-Jul, 6-9 eggs, incubation 27-31 days, young fledge at 6-7 weeks. Nests on ground.

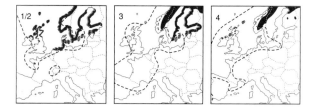

1|2

3

4

1 # Goldeneye

Bucephala clangula

(Wildfowl)

In Britain: Jan-Dec; breeds only in Scotland.
Identification: 46 cm/500-1100 g. Stocky diving duck with high peaked triangular head; male head black with green gloss, roundish white patch behind bill, upperparts black, underparts white, broad white shoulder stripes; female head brown, upperparts pale grey.
Voice: Male rasping *'kraah'* or crooning *'knirr'*; female softer *'krrr'*.
Habitat: Inland lakes, open water in wooded countryside.
Food: Snails, worms, small crustaceans, aquatic insects.
Breeding: May-Jul, 6-11 eggs, incubation 27-32 days, young fledge at 8-9 weeks. Hole nester.

2/3 # Long-tailed Duck

Clangula hyemalis

(Wildfowl)

In Britain: Oct-Apr.
Identification: 53 cm (male), 41 cm (female)/600-900 g. Male in summer (Plate 2 right) and winter (Plate 3) with long tail spike; female in winter plumage with white head, dark crown, grey ear patch, back and breast dark, underparts white; in summer much darker.
Voice: Male a far-carrying *'aulick-a-a-aulick'*; female a hurried quacking.
Habitat: Tundra pools; in winter on the sea. *Food:* Mussels, crabs.
Breeding: Jun-Jul, 5-9 eggs, incubation 23-25 days, young fledge at 5-6 weeks. Nests on ground.

4 # Mandarin

Aix galericulata

(Wildfowl)

In Britain: Jan-Dec; originally escaped from collections.
Identification: 43 cm. Small duck with bright, richly coloured and patterned head, long crest and orange erect 'sails' in the wing (picture on back cover); female grey-brown; white eye-ring extending back towards nape.
Voice: Male a piping *'vrrick'* in flight, female *'ack ack'*.
Habitat: Rivers and lakes in parkland. *Food:* Seeds, fruits, nuts, worms, insects.
Breeding: Apr-Jun, 9-12 eggs, incubation 28-30 days, young fledge at 6 weeks. Hole nester.

1

2

3

1   Goosander   *Mergus merganser*
(Wildfowl)

In Britain: Jan-Dec.
Identification: 66 cm/1.2-2 kg. Largest sawbill; male white with
salmon-pink flush, back black, head and upper neck black with dark
green gloss, mane-like nape, red bill; female head and upper neck brown,
clearly demarcated from grey body feathers. Mane unkempt.
Voice: In courtship male utters a metallic *'kirr korr-kirr kirr korr'*; female
'eckeckeckeck'.
Habitat: Rivers and lakes with clear water and trees on bank.
Food: Fish up to 15 cm long.
Breeding: Apr-Jun, 8-12 eggs, incubation 32-35 days, young fledge at
8-9 weeks. Hole nester.

2   Red-breasted Merganser   *Mergus serrator*
(Wildfowl)

In Britain: Jan-Dec.
Identification: 58 cm/800-1300 g. Approximately Mallard-sized, bill thinner
and more delicate than that of Goosander; double-pointed crest, breast
reddish-brown, flanks pale grey; female very similar to female Goosander,
but the brown of head and upper neck blends into the grey of the body.
Voice: Male cat-like *'yiuv'* or hard *'orrr'*; female *'rokrokrokrok'*.
Habitat: Shallow coastal waters, fjords, inland lakes, rivers.
Food: Fish and crustaceans.
Breeding: May-Jul, 7-12 eggs, incubation 29-35 days, young fledge at
8-9 weeks. Nests on ground.

3   Smew   *Mergus albellus*
(Wildfowl)

In Britain: Nov-Apr.
Identification: 42 cm/550-900 g. Much smaller than Merganser, only the size
of Tufted Duck; male mainly white with some black markings; female crown
and nape rufous-brown, sides of head whitish, upperparts slate grey.
Voice: In courtship male utters a high grating *'krr-eck'*; female a
monosyllabic *'greg'*.
Habitat: Freshwater lakes and pools in well wooded countryside,
flooded forest.
Food: Small fish and aquatic insects.
Breeding: May-Jul, 6-9 eggs, incubation 26-30 days. Hole nester.

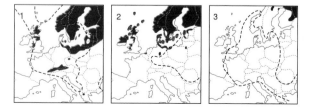

BIRDS OF PREY
Birds of prey in flight

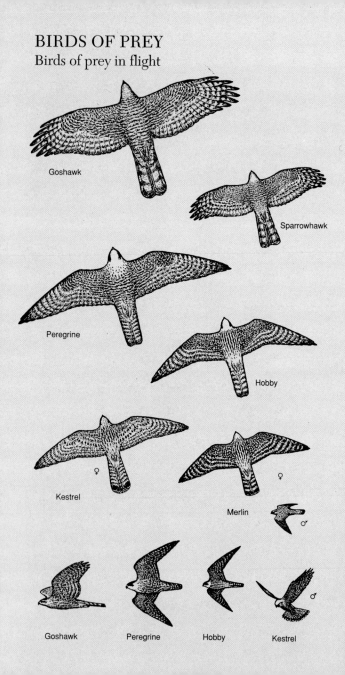

Goshawk

Sparrowhawk

Peregrine

Hobby

Kestrel ♀

Merlin ♀ ♂

Goshawk

Peregrine

Hobby

Kestrel ♂

Buzzard

Honey-buzzard

Black Kite

Red Kite

Marsh Harrier ♂

♀

Montagu's Harrier ♂

♀

1 # Osprey

Pandion haliaetus

(Birds of prey)

In Britain: Apr-Sep.

Identification: 51-58 cm/1.2-2 kg. Medium-sized raptor with white underparts, dark brown upperparts and white head. Sexes similar. Young with crown and nape darker, more strongly streaked, tail feathers more strongly barred.

Flight: Unmistakable through combination of slender profile, long narrow wings, held angled, except when soaring, and its dazzling white underparts. When hunting it flies with slow wingbeats over lakes and rivers. Hovers frequently.

Voice: When breeding mostly short series of notes descending in pitch towards the end *'tyipp-tyipp-tyipp-tyoopp-tyupp-tyupp'*.

Habitat: Forests with plenty of lakes, rivers, sea coasts.

Food: Entirely fish, up to 2 kg in weight.

Breeding: Apr-Jul, 2-4 eggs, incubation 38 days, young fledge at 50-59 days. Nests in tree.

2 # White-tailed Eagle

Haliaeetus albicilla

(Birds of prey)

In Britain: Jan-Dec; extinct, recently reintroduced.

Identification: 69-91 cm/4-7.5 kg. Very large heavily-built eagle with conspicuous yellow bill and short tail. Adults grey-brown with pale head and white tail. Sexes similar. Young darker, lacking colour contrast between head and body, dark tail.

Flight: Broad, plank-like wings, head projecting well and short wedge-shaped tail distinguish the sea eagle in soaring flight. Flapping flight powerful with deep wingbeats.

Voice: In display flight male utters a repeated *'krick-rick-rick-rick'*, female a deeper *'ra-rack-rack-rack'*; other calls *'krau'* or *'ge-ge-ge'*.

Habitat: Sea coasts, large lakes and rivers.

Food: Prefers large fish and water birds (coots, ducks, geese, grebes), also mammals and especially carrion.

Breeding: Feb-Jul, 1-3 eggs, incubation 34-42 days, young fledge at 70-90 days. Nests in tree, or on cliff ledge.

White-tailed Eagle

Osprey

1

Red Kite
Milvus milvus

(Birds of prey)
In Britain: Jan-Dec.
Identification: 61 cm/900-1200 g.
Larger and much more slender than
Buzzard (p. 60); deeply forked,
rusty-red tail; plumage reddish-brown
with pale grey head. Sexes similar.
Flight: Flapping flight buoyant, gull-like,
glides for long periods on angled wings.
Voice: Call a wailing *'hie-hii-hii-hii-hie'*.
Habitat: Old deciduous woodland.
Food: Rodents, birds, carrion.
Breeding: Mar-Jun, 2-3 eggs,
incubation 28-32 days, young fledge at
45-50 days. Nests in tree.

2

Black Kite
Milvus migrans

(Birds of prey)
In Britain: Rare visitor, mainly Apr-Jun.
Identification: 56 cm/700-1000 g. Smaller and stouter than Red Kite,
much darker (blackish-brown), tail only shallowly forked. Sociable.
Flight: Flight not as effortless as Red Kite.
Voice: Call Buzzard-like *'hieh'*; when breeding a whinnying, thin trill.
Habitat: Well wooded countryside with lakes.
Food: Sick and dead fish, young birds, small mammals, carrion.
Breeding: Apr-Jun, 2-3 eggs, incubation 28-32 days, young fledge at
40-45 days. Nests in tree.

3

Short-toed Eagle
Circaetus gallicus

(Birds of prey)
In Britain: Not recorded.
Identification: 63-69 cm/1.4-2.1 kg. Small eagle with robust harrier-like
head and orange-yellow eyes. Sexes similar.
Flight: Buzzard-like silhouette, but with longer tail and more strongly
angled wings. Long glides, hovers frequently.
Voice: When breeding *'kiiyo'* or *'kyi-kyi'*. *Habitat:* Open, dry countryside.
Food: Mainly snakes, also lizards and other reptiles.
Breeding: Apr-Jul, 1 egg, incubation 45-47 days, young fledge at
70-75 days. Nests in tree.

Goshawk

Accipiter gentilis

(Birds of prey)

In Britain: Jan-Dec; scarce, increasing.

Identification: 48-61 cm/700-1200 g. Female Buzzard-sized, male a third smaller, round-winged, long-tailed raptor. Upperparts grey (male) or grey-brown (female), underparts of adults (Plate 1) narrowly barred, in young (Plate 2) with drop-shaped streaking.

Flight: Alternate flapping and gliding, wingbeats more rapid than Buzzard, soaring only in spring display, when the tail is not so strongly fanned as in Buzzard. When hunting birds (such as pigeons) dashing level pursuit-flight.

Voice: Buzzard-like *'hiieh'*, in courtship a repeated rising and falling *'gigigigigi'*; usually silent.

Habitat: Woodland and forest, especially coniferous.

Food: Mammals and birds up to the size of hare or Capercaillie; male hunts mainly birds.

Breeding: Mar-Jul, 3-4 eggs, incubation 35-41 days, young fledge at 38-43 days. Nests in tree.

Sparrowhawk

Accipiter nisus

(Birds of prey)

In Britain: Jan-Dec.

Identification: 28-38 cm/130-320 g. Small version of Goshawk; female size of Kestrel, male only large thrush-sized. Upperparts brown-grey (female) or blue-grey (male), underparts finely barred. Very wary, sits upright, head sunken, with conspicuous shaking of tail after landing.

Flight: Alternate rapid flapping and gliding round bushes and between trees, mostly low to the ground. When displaying male and female climb above the canopy and soar for a short time in upcurrents.

Voice: In display *'giu-giu-giu-giu'*.

Habitat: Woodland with open countryside.

Food: Almost entirely birds, up to the size of Partridge or Woodpigeon, rarely mice.

Breeding: May-Jul, 4-6 eggs, incubation 33-35 days, young fledge at 24-30 days. Nests in tree.

1 Buzzard

Buteo buteo

(Birds of prey)
In Britain: Jan-Dec.
Identification: 51-56 cm/600-1300 g. Plumage varies from dark brown to almost white. Sexes similar. Broad-winged, chunky-looking bird of prey.
Flight: Slow flapping flight with heavy, stiff wingbeats. When soaring the broad wings and strongly spread tail are diagnostic.
Voice: A cat-like *'hiieh'*.
Habitat: Deciduous, mixed and coniferous woodland.
Food: Mice and other small rodents, young birds, reptiles.
Breeding: Apr-Jul, 2-3 eggs, incubation 33-35 days, young fledge at 50-55 days. Nests usually in tree.
Similar species: **Long-legged Buzzard** *Buteo rufinus.* Somewhat larger than Buzzard, tail mostly cinnamon, unbanded. Lives in semi-deserts and mountains of southeast Europe; feeds on small mammals, lizards and snakes.

2 Rough-legged Buzzard

Buteo lagopus

(Birds of prey)
In Britain: Oct-Apr; scarce.
Identification: 51-61 cm/700-1600 g. Somewhat larger than Buzzard. Crown, nape and sides of head always whitish, otherwise, like Buzzard, variable in colour. Sexes similar.
Flight: Longer-winged than Buzzard, tail pale, white rump and broad dark terminal tail band; underwing pale. *Voice:* Similar to Buzzard; seldom calls.
Habitat: Northern tundra; in winter fields and meadows.
Food: Mainly lemmings; in winter quarters as Buzzard.
Breeding: May-Jun, 3-5 eggs, incubation 28-31 days, young fledge at 41-43 days. Nests in tree, on cliff or on ground.

3 Honey-buzzard

Pernis apivorus

(Birds of prey)
In Britain: Apr-Oct; rare breeder.
Identification: 51-58 cm/600-1000 g. Size of Buzzard but more slender. Upperparts dark brown, underparts pale, often with darker markings, very variable. Sexes similar.
Flight: Flapping flight stronger, wingbeats deeper than Buzzard; when soaring narrower wings and long tail with two dark bands help identify.
Voice: Plaintive *'hoodliihooh'*. *Habitat:* Deciduous forest. *Food:* Wasp and bee grubs.
Breeding: May-Jul, 2 eggs, incubation 30-37 days, young fledge at 40-44 days. Nests in tree.

1

2

3

1 Lesser Spotted Eagle

Aquila pomarina

(Birds of prey)

In Britain: Not recorded.

Identification: 61-66 cm/1.1-2 kg. Small eagle. Paler brown than the very similar, but larger Spotted Eagle. Sexes similar. Young uniform chocolate-brown with row of pale spots on the wing-coverts.

Flight: Flight silhouette distinctive, with broad plank-like wings of even width from body to wing-tip.

Voice: Very vocal; in vicinity of nest a repeated '*yup-yup-yup-yupyupyipyipyip*'.

Habitat: Damp woodland bordering meadows.

Food: Mice, rats, moles, frogs, slow-worms, snakes, birds.

Breeding: May-Jul, 2 eggs, incubation 38-41 days, young fledge at 50-55 days. Nests in tree.

2 Spotted Eagle

Aquila clanga

(Birds of prey)

In Britain: Rare vagrant; not recorded since 1915.

Identification: 66-73 cm/1.6-2.3 kg. Larger than Lesser Spotted Eagle. Uniform dark brown. Sexes similar. Young (Plate) brown-black with conspicuous pale spotting, pale V at base of tail.

Flight: Like Lesser Spotted Eagle, but appearing black below, base of primaries pale. *Voice:* A yapping '*kli-kli-kli-kli*'.

Habitat: Extensive woods with heaths and meadows.

Food: Like Lesser Spotted Eagle, but also larger birds (such as coots, ducks, Black Grouse, crows), often hunts by and over water.

Breeding: May-Jul, 1-3 eggs, incubation 42-44 days, young fledge at 60-65 days. Nests in tree.

3 Booted Eagle

Hieraaetus pennatus

(Birds of prey)

In Britain: Not recorded.

Identification: 46-53 cm/600-1100 g. Barely Buzzard-sized small eagle. Two colour morphs: pale form with upperparts grey-brown, underparts white or buff (Plate); dark form uniform dark brown with paler tail. Sexes similar.

Flight: From Buzzard (p. 60) by much narrower wings and longer, less strongly fanned, square-ended tail. *Voice:* Wader-like repeated call; very vocal.

Habitat: Hilly forested countryside (especially oak forest).

Food: Reptiles, birds, small mammals up to ground-squirrel size.

Breeding: May-Jul, 2 eggs, incubation 35-39 days, young fledge at 50-55 days. Nests in tree or on cliff.

1 Bonelli's Eagle

Hieraaetus fasciatus

(Birds of prey)

In Britain: Not recorded.

Identification: 66-74 cm/1.5-2.1 kg. Larger than Buzzard (p. 60). Upperparts dark brown, underparts whitish with dark tear-shaped streaks. Sexes similar.

Flight: Similar silhouette to Short-toed Eagle (p. 56), but longer, narrow tail and well projecting head; dark band across underwing coverts.

Voice: Relatively silent; a laughing *'gyiuuh'*.

Habitat: Dry, mountainous areas with scattered woodland.

Food: Birds, mammals, reptiles.

Breeding: Feb-Apr, 2 eggs, incubation 37-40 days, young fledge at 58-61 days. Nests in tree or on cliff.

2 Imperial Eagle

Aquila heliaca

(Birds of prey)

In Britain: Not recorded.

Identification: 78-83 cm/2.5-4 kg. A little smaller, stockier and shorter-tailed than Golden Eagle. Uniform dark brown with white shoulder patches. Spanish race with white carpal (Plate).

Flight: Recalls White-tailed Eagle with its broad, plank-like wings.

Voice: Harsh Raven-like *'krock-krock-krock'*.

Habitat: Open plains with scattered copses, wooded steppes.

Food: Mainly small mammals, rarely birds, often carrion.

Breeding: Mar-May, 2-3 eggs, incubation 43 days, young fledge at 65-77 days. Nests in tree.

3 Golden Eagle

Aquila chrysaetos

(Birds of prey)

In Britain: Jan-Dec.

Identification: 75-88 cm/3-6.6 kg. Large powerful eagle with dark brown plumage, crown and nape golden-yellow. Sexes similar, but female larger. Young blackish-brown with white patch at base of primaries. Hunts by quartering ground in low flight, using cover.

Flight: The long, not especially broad wings are narrowed where they join the body; tail medium long, gently rounded, with pale base in young.

Voice: Buzzard-like *'hiieh'* (rarely calls).

Habitat: Extensive varied forested and mountainous country.

Food: Mammals up to fawn size, birds up to size of Capercaillie; carrion.

Breeding: Mar-Jun, 2 eggs, incubation 43-45 days, young (usually only one) fledge at 65-70 days. Nests on cliff or in tree.

1 Lammergeier

Gypaetus barbatus

(Birds of prey)

In Britain: Not recorded.

Identification: 102-114 cm/5-7 kg. Very large, rather slender vulture, upperparts dark, underparts pale, head and neck rusty, black 'beard'. Sexes similar.

Flight: Falcon-like silhouette; tail long, wedge-shaped.

Voice: In display a high-pitched piping *'fiiiy'*.

Habitat: High mountains at and above the tree-line.

Food: Mainly bones and tortoises, which it drops from a height on to rocky ground to break open; meat, a little carrion.

Breeding: Dec-Mar, 1-2 eggs, incubation 55-60 days, young fledge at 110 days. Nests on cliff.

2 Egyptian Vulture

Neophron percnopterus

(Birds of prey)

In Britain: Very rare vagrant (2 records).

Identification: 56-66 cm/1.8-2.4 kg. Dirty-white with black flight feathers, facial skin yellow. Sexes similar. Young dark brown.

Flight: Long, narrow pointed wings and wedge-shaped tail.

Voice: Grunting whistling notes, though normally silent.

Habitat: Open plains, mountainous country; near human settlement.

Food: Carrion, scraps of meat, excrement.

Breeding: Mar-May, 2 eggs, incubation 42 days, young fledge at 75-90 days. Nests on cliff.

3 Griffon Vulture

Gyps fulvus

(Birds of prey)

In Britain: Very rare vagrant (3 records).

Identification: 97-104 cm/6.5-11 kg. Large, pale sandy wings and tail dark brown, bare goose-like neck, white ruff. Young darker, neck-ruff brown.

Flight: Broad plank-like wings, soars with well-fingered spread primaries; tail short and square. *Voice:* When excited at carrion, a hard *'gegegeg'*.

Habitat: Arid plains, high mountains.

Food: Corpses of large mammals, favours the entrails.

Breeding: Feb-May, 1 egg, incubation 47-54 days, young fledge at 110-120 days. Nests on cliff.

Similar species: **Black Vulture** *Aegypius monachus*. A little larger than Griffon Vulture; plumage uniform dark brown, head pale with bare bluish skin and dark area around eyes. Small numbers left in remote wooded mountain areas of Spain and southeast Europe. May attack live prey.

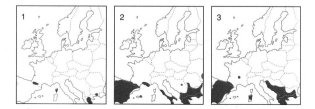

1

2

3

1 Marsh Harrier *Circus aeruginosus*

(Birds of prey)

In Britain: Jan-Dec, mostly Mar-Oct.

Identification: 48-56 cm/400-800 g. Size of Buzzard (p. 60) but much more slender, narrower-winged and longer-tailed. Male mainly brown with pale tail; female and young with cream-coloured head.

Flight: Gliding flight with wings held in shallow 'V', wavering.

Voice: In display flight male utters a Lapwing-like squawking '*kuih*'; alarm-call '*kekekeke*'.

Habitat: Reedbeds. *Food:* Fish, frogs, reptiles, birds, small rodents, young hares.

Breeding: Apr-Jun, 3-6 eggs, incubation 31-38 days, young fledge at 38-40 days. Nests on ground in reeds.

2/3 Hen Harrier *Circus cyaneus*

(Birds of prey)

In Britain: Jan-Dec.

Identification: 43-51 cm/300-550 g. Smaller and more slender than Marsh Harrier. Male (Plate 3) pale grey with white belly; female (Plate 2) brown with banded tail and white rump. Young like female.

Flight: Broader-winged than Montagu's Harrier; effortless flight low over fields and moorland, gliding and soaring on wings raised in 'V'.

Voice: In display flight male calls '*gye gye gye*'; alarm-call '*keckeckeck*'.

Habitat: Open countryside with meadows, fields, bogs and moorland.

Food: Small mammals and birds up to Partridge size.

Breeding: May-Jul, 3-6 eggs, incubation 29-37 days, young fledge at 31-40 days. Nests on ground.

4 Montagu's Harrier *Circus pygargus*

(Birds of prey)

In Britain: Apr-Sep; rare breeding bird.

Identification: 41-46 cm/230-430 g. Smaller and more slender than Hen Harrier. Male bluish ash-grey with black bars on wings and rusty streaking on white underparts. Female like female Hen Harrier, but with smaller white rump-patch, narrower winged. Young like female.

Flight: Like Hen Harrier, but wings narrower and more pointed.

Voice: In display flight male calls '*kekekek*'; female '*pi-eh*'.

Habitat: Damp areas with wet meadows, marshes and reedbeds, cereal fields.

Food: Small mammals and young birds, also lizards and insects.

Breeding: May-Jul, 3-6 eggs, incubation 28-30 days, young fledge at 35-40 days. Nests on ground.

1

2|3

4

1 # Peregrine

Falco peregrinus

(Falcons)

In Britain: Jan-Dec.

Identification: 38-48 cm/550-1100 g. Large compact, sharp-winged and short-tailed falcon; upperparts slate-grey, underparts whitish with narrow barring; top of head and moustache black. Sexes similar, but females mostly darker and appreciably larger.

Flight: Flies with rapid shallow wingbeats, interrupted by short glides, occasionally soars on upcurrents. Silhouette anchor-like.

Voice: Commonest utterance when breeding is given by both sexes, a plaintive, ringing, extended, repeated *'gehiih'*.

Habitat: Open countryside, scattered woodland on plains and in mountains, tundra, semi-deserts.

Food: Almost entirely birds (larks, thrushes, pigeons, gulls, ducks), which it catches in dashing pursuit flight.

Breeding: Apr-Jul, 3-5 eggs, incubation 28-32 days, young fledge at 35-42 days. Nests on rock ledge or in tree.

adult   young

2 # Lanner

(Falcons)

Falco biarmicus

In Britain: Not recorded.

Identification: 43 cm/500-900 g. Size of Peregrine, but slimmer, longer-tailed, wings not so pointed. Coloured like pale Peregrine; upperparts slate-grey, crown and nape pale rufous, moustache narrower than in Peregrine, underparts cream-coloured with rusty tinge, spotted black. Sexes similar. Upperparts of young browner, and with very coarse drop-shaped spotting on underparts.

Flight: Silhouette differs from that of Peregrine in being slimmer, longer-tailed and with less pointed wings. Flies with slower wingbeats.

Voice: Less vocal than Peregrine; usual call soft, also a harsh *'ki ki ki ki ki'*.

Habitat: The southern European race of the Lanner (*feldeggi*) frequents mainly cliffs and gorges.

Food: Almost exclusively birds such as Rock Partridge, Rock Dove, sandgrouse, Lesser Kestrel.

Breeding: Mar-May, 3-4 eggs, incubation 31-35 days, young fledge at 45 days. Crag nester.

1 Saker

Falco cherrug

(Falcons)

In Britain: Not recorded.

Identification: 46 cm/700-1300 g. A little larger than Peregrine (p. 70); upperparts dark brown, head pale with whitish crown, moustache indistinct.

Flight: From Peregrine by broader wings and longer tail.

Voice: Call *'iyek iyek iyek'*; in display a rising *'geck geck geck'*.

Habitat: Wooded and dry steppes, semi-deserts.

Food: Small mammals (mainly ground-squirrels), birds up to the size of ducks.

Breeding: Apr-Jun, 3-5 eggs, incubation 28-30 days, young fledge at 40-45 days. Nest in tree or on cliff.

2 Hobby

Falco subbuteo

(Falcons)

In Britain: Apr-Oct.

Identification: 30-36 cm/175-300 g. Recalls Peregrine (p. 70), but smaller, more graceful and slender, with longer, narrower wings. Upperparts dark slate-grey, underparts white with bold black streaking, rusty 'trousers'.

Flight: Flight silhouette recalls Swift with its narrow sickle-shaped wings.

Voice: *'kiukiukiu'* or *'kikikiki'*.

Habitat: Open woods on dry soils, farmland.

Food: Birds and flying insects.

Breeding: Jun-Aug, 2-4 eggs, incubation 28 days, young fledge at 28-32 days. Nests in tree.

3/4 Red-footed Falcon

Falco vespertinus

(Falcons)

In Britain: May-Jun; rare visitor.

Identification: 30 cm/130-190 g. Smaller than Kestrel (p. 74). Male (Plate 3) dark grey with rusty red 'trousers'; female (Plate 4) rusty buff, lightly streaked on underparts, back ash-grey, barred.

Flight: Silhouette similar to Hobby, but longer-tailed; often hovers.

Voice: Very vocal; high-pitched Kestrel-like *'kikikiki'*.

Habitat: Open countryside with scattered copses. *Food:* Mainly insects.

Breeding: May-Jul, 3-5 eggs, incubation 22-23 days, young fledge at 26-30 days. Nests in tree.

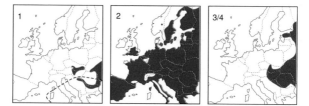

1

2

3|4

1 Merlin

Falco columbarius

(Falcons)

In Britain: Jan-Dec.

Identification: 27-33 cm/160-210 g. Smaller than Kestrel; male upperparts slaty grey, nape rusty, underparts pale rusty with darker streaking; female upperparts dark brown, underparts whitish.

Flight: From Kestrel by shorter tail, from Hobby (p. 72) by broader wings and stockier body. *Voice:* Similar to Kestrel '*kikikiki*'.

Habitat: Open countryside with few trees, moorland, young forestry plantations.

Food: Birds up to thrush size, occasionally mice.

Breeding: May-Jul, 4-5 eggs, incubation 28-32 days, young fledge at 25-27 days. Nests on ground, in tree or on rock ledge.

2 Kestrel

Falco tinnunculus

(Falcons)

In Britain: Jan-Dec.

Identification: 34 cm/150-280 g. Male with crown and cheeks blue-grey, back rufous with broad black spots, tail ash-grey; female with head and back cinnamon, tail red-brown, banded.

Flight: Flies with rapid, shallow wingbeats; hovers frequently.

Voice: A high '*kikikikiki*'; when near nest a long whimpering '*vriiiiiih*'.

Habitat: Catholic, from sea coast to high mountains, with exception of closed forest; villages, towns.

Food: Mice, young birds, large insects.

Breeding: Apr-Jul, 4-6 eggs, incubation 27-31 days, young fledge at 28-32 days. Nests on rock ledge, building or in tree.

3 Lesser Kestrel

Falco naumanni

(Falcons)

In Britain: Rare vagrant.

Identification: 30 cm/130-180 g. Very similar to Kestrel, but a little smaller; rufous upperparts of the male unspotted, head and tail brighter blue-grey; female very difficult to tell from female Kestrel, but claws pale horn-coloured. Very sociable.

Flight: Kestrel-like, but lighter, less erratic.

Voice: A husky rattling '*khe khe khe*' or '*khitschit*'.

Habitat: Warm dry open countryside. *Food:* Chiefly grasshoppers and beetles.

Breeding: May-Jun, 3-6 eggs, incubation 28-29 days, young fledge at 28 days. Nests on rocks, walls, sandstone cliffs. Colonial nester.

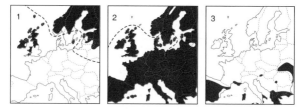

1   Eagle Owl *Bubo bubo*
(Owls)

In Britain: Rare vagrant in 19th century.

Identification: 66-71 cm/2000-3000 g. Largest European owl; powerful, stocky jizz with long feather 'ears' sticking out horizontally, and large orange-red eyes; legs and feet feathered; plumage yellow-brown, upperparts brown-black spotted, underparts streaked and spotted similarly; pale underwing. Female a little bigger, otherwise sexes similar. Active at dusk and by night; hunts in low flight or from a lookout post.

Voice: Female in spring utters a hoarse, nasal '*khriei*'.
Song: far-carrying muffled disyllabic '*uuo*' or '*hohoho*', repeated at 10 second intervals.

Habitat: Mostly river valleys with rock faces in well wooded countryside, hills; hunts mainly in open countryside.

Food: Mammals ranging in size from field mouse to hare, often brown rats, hedgehogs; birds up to size of Capercaillie.

Breeding: Feb-Jul, 2-5 eggs, incubation 31-36 days, young fledge from about 50 days. Cliff nester, occasionally in trees or on the ground.

2   Snowy Owl *Nyctea scandiaca*
(Owls)

In Britain: Rare visitor; bred Shetland 1967-75.

Identification: 55-66 cm/1.7-2.3 kg. Almost Eagle Owl size, white with round head and gleaming yellow eyes; legs and toes strongly feathered. Male almost entirely white, female larger, usually strongly barred with dark brown. Young dark brown with dirty white narrow barring. Flight Buzzard-like, glides a great deal on long, rounded wings. Mainly diurnal, also active at dusk; sit-and-wait hunter from ground or low perch.

Voice: When agitated female gives a cackling or shrill screech; alarm call a hard '*krih*'; when breeding, a far-carrying, repeated harsh booming '*vou*' or '*khruh*'.

Habitat: Arctic tundra, mountain tundra.

Food: Mainly lemmings; other small rodents, blue hares, grouse.

Breeding: May-Jul, 4-8 eggs, incubation 32-33 days, young leave nest at about 3 weeks, can fly at 6-7 weeks. Nests on the ground.

1 Barn Owl

Tyto alba

(Owls)

In Britain: Jan-Dec.

Identification: 34 cm/350 g. Medium-sized, pale owl, lacking feather ears, with a heart-shaped facial disc, and dark eyes; upperparts grey, mixed with golden brown spots. In flight very long wings obvious. Usually nocturnal, may hunt by day in winter.

Voice: Alarm call a short shrill *'khrii'*; also snoring and hissing noises. Song: two second long purring screech.

Habitat: Varied open farmland.

Food: Small mammals, mostly field mice, also shrews; birds, amphibians, insects.

Breeding: Mar-Oct, 4-7 eggs, incubation 30-34 days, young fledge at 44-67 days; 1 or 2 broods per year. Nests in buildings, rarely in holes in rocks.

2 Long-eared Owl

Asio otus

(Owls)

In Britain: Jan-Dec.

Identification: 36 cm/280 g. Smaller and slimmer than Tawny Owl (p. 82); long feather ears, orange-yellow eyes, conspicuous, well defined facial disc; plumage colour of bark. Female often darker than male. In flight long rather pointed wings. Active at dusk and by night; in winter often in loose groups.

Voice: Alarm call *'uek'*, sometimes repeated; hissing *'khviiu'*. Song of male: muffled soft *'huh'*. Young a plaintive *'stsieh'*.

Habitat: Woodland on the edge of open country, copses; in winter also settlements.

Food: Mostly field mice, other small rodents, shrews, birds.

Breeding: Mar-Jun, 3-6 eggs, incubation 27-28 days, young leave nest at 18-25 days, fledge from 30 days. Breeds mainly in abandoned crows' nests.

3 Scops Owl

Otus scops

(Owls)

In Britain: Rare vagrant.

Identification: 19 cm/90 g. Small, slim bark-coloured owl with conspicuous feather ears, yellow eyes and inconspicuous facial disc. Sexes similar. Strictly nocturnal.

Voice: Alarm call a long piercing *'piiie'*. Song a monotonous repeated *'diu'*; female call higher-pitched.

Habitat: Orchards, olive groves, parkland, avenues of trees; also villages and towns.

Food: Large insects, spiders, worms, mice, small birds.

Breeding: Apr-Jun, 3-5 eggs, incubation 24-29 days, young fledge at 21-29 days. Usually nests in tree holes.

Short-eared Owl

Asio flammeus

(Owls)

In Britain: Jan-Dec.

Identification: 38 cm/380 g. More stocky and longer-winged than
Long-eared Owl (p. 78); only very small, usually concealed feather ears,
conspicuous pale facial disc, eyes yellow; upperparts mottled black-brown
and cream, underparts pale yellowish-brown, strongly streaked
black-brown on throat and breast. Female on the whole darker than
male. Diurnal as well as nocturnal. Often sits on posts, rarely in trees.

Flight: Underwing whitish with blackish tips and dark carpal mark; flight
soft and wavering with slow, deep wingbeats; quarters the ground low,
often hovers; on breeding territory Buzzard-like circling (Plate 2); display
flight includes wing-clapping.

Voice: In spring, when threatened, male utters a yapping '*kver-vek-vek*',
female '*varr*'. Song of male: 8-12 syllable '*bu-bu-bu*'.

Habitat: Open marshy areas, moorland, damp meadows, dunes.

Food: Chiefly voles, mice, rats, shrews, birds.

Breeding: Apr-Jul, 4-8 eggs, incubation 24-28 days, young leave nest at
12-17 days, fledge from 24 days. Nests on ground in low vegetation.

Hawk Owl

Surnia ulula

(Owls)

In Britain: Rare vagrant.

Identification: 38 cm/300 g. Long wedge-shaped tail, white facial disc,
broadly edged with black, pale yellow eyes; upperparts dark grey-brown,
spotted with white, underparts barred, sparrowhawk-like. Sexes similar.
Young much paler, upperparts with little spotting. Mostly active by day
and at dusk; often sits on tree stumps, wags its tail.

Voice: When disturbed a falcon-like ringing '*kvikvikvi*', '*kvitt kvitt*', yapping '*geff
geff*'. Territorial song of male: 2-3 second
long trilling '*u-u-uuuuuu*' or '*giugiugiu-
iuiuiuiu*'; voice of female harsher.

Habitat: Open conifer, mixed and birch
woods bordering open country.

Food: Chiefly voles, mice, shrews, birds.

Breeding: Apr-Jun, 3-13 eggs,
incubation 25-30 days, young fledge
at 30 days. Nests in tree holes or uses
old bird of prey nest.

1 · Tengmalm's Owl
(Owls)

Aegolius funereus

In Britain: Rare vagrant.
Identification: 25 cm/male 100 g, female 160 g. Larger and longer-tailed than Little Owl, with large head and pale facial disc, arched high over the yellow eyes; upperparts dark grey-brown with large white spots, underparts paler. Young chocolate brown. Active at dusk and by night.
Voice: Alarm call a snapping *'tsiuck'*. Territorial song of male 1-2 second long rising utterance of 5-9 separate repeated notes *'huhuhuhuhu'*.
Habitat: Conifer and mixed woods with Black Woodpecker holes, nestboxes.
Food: Small rodents, shrews, small birds.
Breeding: Mar-Jun, 3-6 eggs, incubation 26-29 days, young fledge at 30-32 days. Hole nester.

2 · Tawny Owl
(Owls)

Strix aluco

In Britain: Jan-Dec.
Identification: 38 cm/male 450 g, female 550 g. Large, round head with large black eyes; plumage rufous brown to grey, streaked darker; streaks on underparts with 'cross branches'. Active at dusk and by night; often suns itself.
Voice: Call *'ku-vitt'* (especially the young), alarm *'uett'*. Song: soft tremulous *'guuoh gu gur-ruuh'*.
Habitat: Deciduous and mixed woods, parkland.
Food: Small mammals, birds, frogs.
Breeding: Feb-Jun, 2-5 eggs, incubation 28-30 days, young leave nest at 25-30 days, fly a week later. Hole nester.

3 · Little Owl
(Owls)

Athene noctua

In Britain: Jan-Dec; originally introduced.
Identification: 22 cm/170 g. Small, flat-headed and short-tailed owl; large pale yellow eyes, indistinct facial disc; upperparts brown with white spots, underparts yellowish-white with brown streaking. Young paler. Active both by night and day; often sits on telegraph poles; bobs when agitated.
Voice: Alarm call a short *'kiu'*, sometimes repeated. Territorial song of male a soft upslurred *'uuhg'*, repeated 10 to 20 times a minute.
Habitat: Varied open farmland, orchards; also in villages.
Food: Large insects, spiders, mice, small birds, reptiles.
Breeding: Apr-Jun, 3-5 eggs, incubation 24-28 days, young fledge at 34 days. Hole nester.

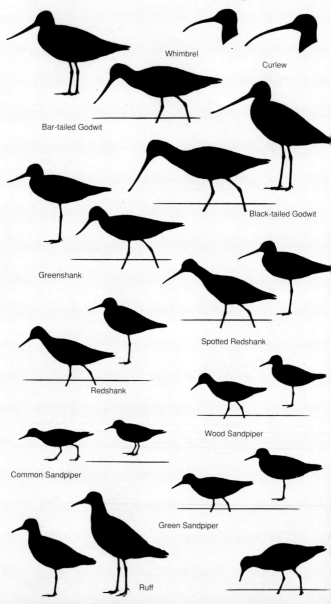

WADERS
Silhouettes of birds at rest and moving

Whimbrel

Curlew

Bar-tailed Godwit

Black-tailed Godwit

Greenshank

Spotted Redshank

Redshank

Wood Sandpiper

Common Sandpiper

Green Sandpiper

Ruff

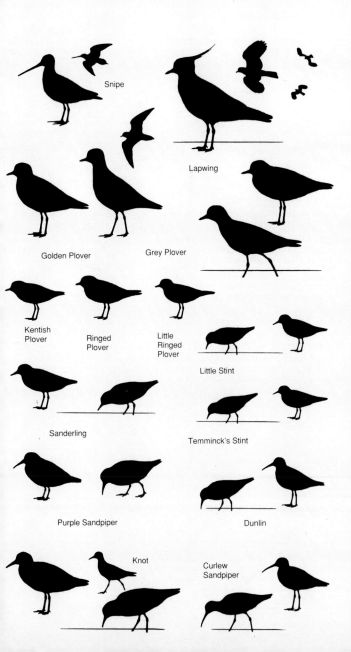

Snipe

Lapwing

Golden Plover

Grey Plover

Kentish
Plover

Ringed
Plover

Little
Ringed
Plover

Little Stint

Sanderling

Temminck's Stint

Purple Sandpiper

Dunlin

Knot

Curlew
Sandpiper

1 Great Bustard
Otis tarda

(Bustards)

In Britain: Rare vagrant; former breeder.

Identification: Male 102 cm/12 kg; female 76 cm/3.8 kg. Very large, thickset walking bird with strong legs, turkey-like appearance; upperparts reddish-brown, barred black, head and neck whitish-grey, underparts white. Male with rufous breast band, long white beard of feathers at base of bill and with thicker neck than female. Runs with head raised and body held horizontal; goose-like flight with slow, powerful wingbeats; spectacular display of male: it turns its white underwing and undertail coverts partly upwards, raises tail on to its back, inflates its neck sac like a balloon and lays its head back into its plumage; then turns jerkily in a circle.

courtship display of Great Bustard

Voice: When displaying male utters a muffled '*umb*' or '*khaub*'; female mostly a plaintive '*veiii*'.

Habitat: Steppes; wide open cultivated steppe.

Food: Shoots, leaves and seeds of steppe plants and farmland weeds; insects, earthworms, lizards, mice.

Breeding: Apr-Jul, 2-3 eggs, incubation 21-26 days, young fly at about 5 weeks. Nests on ground.

2 Little Bustard
Tetrax tetrax

(Bustards)

In Britain: Rare vagrant.

Identification: 43 cm/800 g. Small bustard with long legs, thick neck and short bill; male with conspicuous black-and-white neck-pattern, cheeks and throat grey; female barred on breast and flanks. Very shy, but may be found among grazing cattle; conspicuous display: male stretches up in the grass, calls at intervals, snapping back its head and neck, followed by a leap and two powerful wing flaps; display flight low over the ground with downcurved, vibrating wings and head raised high; whistling wing noise of male.

Voice: Display call of the male a short hard '*ptrr*' or '*trrrt*'.

Habitat: Open grassy steppes in rolling countryside; varied farmland.

Food: Grass, seeds, insects, worms, small vertebrates.

Breeding: May-Jul, 2-4 eggs, incubation 20-22 days, young fly at about 4 weeks. Nests on ground.

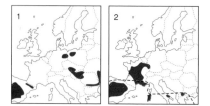

1 Water Rail

Rallus aquaticus

(Crakes and rails)

In Britain: Jan-Dec.

Identification: 28 cm/120 g. Slim bird; long red bill, long reddish legs; upperparts dark brown with black streaking, sides of head and underparts slate-grey, undertail-coverts gleaming white, flanks barred black-and-white. Remains hidden in tall waterside vegetation; usually runs from danger.

Voice: Very noisy; piglet-like descending *'kruih kruih kruih'*, also *'gip gip gip'* and growling or rasping noises. Courtship song a series of short *'tiuk'* notes.

Habitat: Dense reedbeds by water, in ditches.

Food: Aquatic insects, tadpoles, worms, frogs.

Breeding: Apr-Jul, 7-10 eggs, incubation 19-20 days, young fly at 3-4 weeks. Nests in dense waterside vegetation.

2 Spotted Crake

Porzana porzana

(Crakes and rails)

In Britain: Apr-Oct; rare.

Identification: 23 cm/80 g. Song Thrush-sized stocky rail with short bill and greenish legs; plumage brownish with fine white spots; undertail-coverts creamy yellow. Sexes similar. Rarely seen, crepuscular; remains even more hidden than Water Rail.

Voice: Courtship song of male: loud monotonous *'huitt huitt'*.

Habitat: Grassy wet meadows, overgrown ditches.

Food: Mostly small beetles, flies, dragonfly larvae.

Breeding: Apr-Jul, 8-12 eggs, incubation 18-19 days, young independent at about 40 days. Nest often on grass tussock.

3 Little Crake

Porzana parva

(Crakes and rails)

In Britain: Rare vagrant.

Identification: 19 cm/55 g. Somewhat smaller than Starling; bill greenish with red base; upperparts with few white spots, inconspicuous flank barring; underparts slate grey, in female pale buff. Shy, remains well hidden; climbs and swims well.

Voice: Courtship song of male an accelerating series of *'quek quek quek'* notes, dropping in pitch; female *'puck puck purrr'*, *'kiukrirr'*.

Habitat: Dense reedbeds and stands of reedmace.

Food: Fly larvae, snails, worms.

Breeding: May-Jul, 4-8 eggs, incubation 21 days, young fledge at 45-50 days. Nests in reeds.

1 Baillon's Crake

Porzana pusilla

(Crakes and rails)

In Britain: Rare vagrant.

Identification: 18 cm/30-50 g. Very small rail with uniform green bill; legs pale olive-green; upperparts brown to chestnut with many white streaks and small spots; sides of head, throat and underparts slate-grey, flanks and undertail coverts barred black-and-white. Female similar to male, but a little paler and less richly coloured. Very hard to observe.

Voice: At start of nesting, male utters a far-carrying wooden croaking *'rrrrrr'* or *'tiurri'*, reminiscent of the call of drake Garganey (p. 40) or marsh frog, each phrase lasting 1 to 3 seconds.

Habitat: Meadows of dense sedge and sweet-grass standing in 10-50 cm of water at the edge of pools, lakes, rivers.

Food: Insects, worms, snails, tender plant material.

Breeding: May-Jul, 6-9 eggs, incubation 17-20 days, young able to fly at 5 weeks. Nest on sedge tussock, in thick vegetation.

2 Corncrake

Crex crex

(Crakes and rails)

In Britain: Apr-Oct; now very uncommon.

Identification: 27 cm/150 g. Recalling Grey Partridge (p. 148), but smaller and slimmer; upperparts yellowish-brown with dark feather centres, wing-coverts rufous, breast and sides of head grey, throat whitish, flanks and undertail broadly barred chestnut; relatively short, yellowish bill. Sexes similar. In flight no wing noise, weak wingbeats, no glides; from flying partridge also by dangling legs and rufous wing-coverts as well as lack of red in tail; runs very rapidly through thick vegetation, head and neck held horizontal, without disturbing the stems.

Voice: Courtship song of male: very characteristic and persistent, day and night, audible up to 1 km away, a rasping *'rerrp rerrp'*.

Habitat: Wet meadows, grassy pastures, clover and lucerne fields, flowery meadows; occasionally cornfields, rape and potato fields.

Food: Beetles, dragonflies, flies, worms, snails, small invertebrates.

Breeding: May-Jul, 7-12 eggs, incubation 16-19 days, young fledge at about 5 weeks. Nests in shallow hollow on ground.

Corncrake in flight

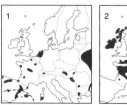

1   Coot   *Fulica atra*

(Crakes and rails)

In Britain: Jan-Dec.

Identification: 38 cm/700 g. Almost duck-sized, dumpy, black; bill and frontal shield white; toes lobed. Sexes similar. When swimming nods head rhythmically (but much less than Moorhen); outside breeding season often in large flocks on lakes. Dives with a small leap.

Voice: Hard *'pix'*, *'dp'*, *'pssi'*; female a barking *'kiv'*.

Habitat: Waters with rich aquatic vegetation.

Food: Aquatic plants, reed shoots, grass, insects.

Breeding: Apr-Jul, 5-10 eggs, incubation 23-24 days, young independent at about 8 weeks. Usually builds floating nest.

2   Moorhen   *Gallinula chloropus*

(Crakes and rails)

In Britain: Jan-Dec.

Identification: 33 cm/300 g. Small, blackish; legs and toes long, greenish; bill red with yellow tip, red frontal shield; outer undertail coverts gleaming white. Sexes similar. Young inconspicuous grey-brown. Runs and swims with rhythmical head movements and frantic tail twitching.

Voice: Alarm call a sharp *'kiurrk'* or *'kirreck'*.

Habitat: Water-bodies with thickly vegetated banks.

Food: Aquatic plants, grass, insects, tadpoles.

Breeding: Apr-Jul, 4-10 eggs, incubation 19-22 days, young fledge at 40-50 days; 1-3 broods per annum. Nest floating or in thick waterside vegetation.

3   Crane   *Grus grus*

(Cranes)

In Britain: Jan-Dec; rare.

Identification: 114 cm/5.5 kg. Very large, mainly grey; relatively short, strong bill; red patch on back of head. Sexes similar. Very shy and wary; walks majestically; remarkable dance ('crane dance') on breeding grounds and at traditional stopover sites on migration; birds dance round each other with outspread wings, leaping into the air and bowing.

Voice: Loud trumpeting *'kruh-krui-kruh'*, especially at dawn and when taking flight.

Habitat: Extensive marshes and bogs.

Food: Seeds, plant material, potatoes, insects, snails, small vertebrates.

Breeding: Apr-Jun, 2(-3) eggs, incubation 29-30 days, young fly at 9-10 weeks. Nests on ground.

1 Oystercatcher

Haematopus ostralegus

(Oystercatchers)

In Britain: Jan-Dec.

Identification: 43 cm/600 g. Large, stocky shorebird with powerful red legs and long orange-red bill; head, breast and upperparts black, underparts white; eyes red. In winter plumage white band across throat to sides of neck. Sexes similar. In flight white wing-bar, white tail with broad black terminal band. Very sociable.

Voice: Piercing *'kliep kliep'*; when threatened *'gleea gleea'*.

Habitat: Coasts and beaches of all kinds, including inland waters.

Food: Mussels, crustaceans, snails, lugworms.

Breeding: Apr-Jul, 3 eggs, incubation 26-28 days, young fledge at 32-35 days. Nests on ground.

2 Black-winged Stilt

Himantopus himantopus

(Stilts and avocets)

In Britain: Apr-Sep; rare visitor, has bred.

Identification: 38 cm/200 g. Graceful wader with fine black bill and very long, thin, red legs; back and wings black, otherwise white; male blackish on top and back of head, white outside breeding season. Female like non-breeding male, but with brownish-black upperparts.

Voice: Alarm call a shrill *'kvip'*, *'kvivip'*; also *'diua'*, *'gick'*.

Habitat: Mostly saline marshes.

Food: Insects, small crustaceans, tadpoles, fish.

Breeding: Apr-Jun, 3-4 eggs, incubation 22-24 days, young fledge at 28-30 days. Colonial breeder; nests on ground.

3 Avocet

Recurvirostra avosetta

(Stilts and avocets)

In Britain: Jan-Dec.

Identification: 43 cm/300 g. Large, elegant black-and-white shorebird with long blue-grey legs and upturned black bill. Sexes similar. In flight pure white below apart from black primaries. When feeding, sweeps head from side to side; very sociable.

Voice: Soft *'pluit'*, *'pliewt'*; alarm call *'blik-blik-blik'*.

Habitat: Muddy bays, lagoons, saltpans.

Food: Small crustaceans, worms, aquatic insects.

Breeding: Apr-Jul, 4 eggs, incubation 24-25 days, young fledge at 35-40 days. Colonial breeder; nests in shallow hollow on ground.

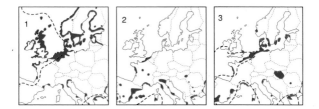

2|3

1 Ringed Plover · *Charadrius hiaticula*

(Plovers)

In Britain: Jan-Dec.

Identification: 19 cm/65 g. Small dumpy-looking wader; legs and bill orange-yellow, bill tip black; in flight conspicuous white wingbar; forehead white, broad black breast-band. In non-breeding plumage, white patch behind eye, loses black markings on head and neck. Sexes similar. Runs very rapidly, stops suddenly and bows forward.

Voice: 'tewit'; in song flight 't'viueh t'viueh t'viueh', 'driu driu driu'.

Habitat: Sea shore, mountain tundra; small numbers inland.

Food: Insects, small crustaceans, worms, snails.

Breeding: Apr-Jul, 3-4 eggs, incubation 21-28 days, young fledge at 21-25 days; double-brooded. Nests in scrape on ground.

2 Little Ringed Plover · *Charadrius dubius*

(Plovers)

In Britain: Apr-Oct.

Identification: 15 cm/40 g. Smaller than Ringed Plover; slim black bill, forehead with more black than Ringed Plover, narrow black breast-band, lemon yellow eye-ring, pale yellowish legs; lacks white wingbar. Runs rapidly.

Voice: High piping 'piu', 'diu'; in display an accelerating trill 'griu griu griu', 'tria tria tria'.

Habitat: Gravel and sand banks on rivers and lakes; gravel- and sand-pits.

Food: Beetles, crustaceans, snails, worms.

Breeding: Apr-Jul, 4 eggs, incubation 22-28 days, young fledge at 24-27 days. Nests in scrape on ground.

3 Kentish Plover · *Charadrius alexandrinus*

(Plovers)

In Britain: Mar-Sep; rare migrant, former breeder.

Identification: 16 cm/50 g. Small, pale, relatively long-legged 'ringed plover'; legs and bill blackish; narrow black (brown in female) incomplete breast-band, broken in middle. Female less contrasting. In flight white wing-bar obvious. Male in spring with orange-rufous hind-crown. In non-breeding plumage like breeding female. Runs long distances.

Voice: 'pewit', 'giugiug'; trilling song flight.

Habitat: Sandy beaches, saltpans.

Food: Worms, insects, crustaceans.

Breeding: Apr-Jul, 3 eggs, incubation 23-29 days, young fledge at 30-40 days. Nests on ground.

1

2

3

1 Golden Plover

Pluvialis apricaria

(Plovers)

In Britain: Jan-Dec.

Identification: 28 cm/190 g. Large, roundish-looking plover with black upperparts finely mottled greenish-yellow; underparts and face according to race more or less black, in non-breeding plumage dirty white. Sexes similar. In flight pointed wings, underwing white. Very sociable, often in company with Lapwings.

Voice: Soft piping *'diuh'*, *'tliuh'*; when agitated *'tlew-i'*; song flight *'tew-tew-tewdiu-tewdiu-tewdiu'*.

Habitat: Heaths and moors, tundra; on migration often in fields and meadows.

Food: Insects, spiders, small snails, berries.

Breeding: Apr-Jul, 3-4 eggs, incubation 27-30 days, young fledge at 30-33 days. Nests in hollow on ground.

2 Grey Plover

Pluvialis squatarola

(Plovers)

In Britain: Jan-Dec; does not breed.

Identification: 29 cm/220 g. Similar to Golden Plover, but rather larger and stockier, with stout bill; upperparts without yellow and green tones. In non-breeding plumage grey rather than yellowish; conspicuous white stripe over eye. In flight black 'armpits' stand out; often singly.

Voice: Mostly in flight, a melancholy 3 syllable *'tli-oo-i'*.

Habitat: Arctic tundra, on migration on muddy shores.

Food: Insects, mussels, snails, lugworms.

Breeding: May-Jul, 4 eggs, incubation 27 days, young independent at 4-5 weeks. Nests in hollow on ground.

3 Dotterel

Charadrius morinellus

(Plovers)

In Britain: May-Oct.

Identification: 20-22 cm/100-120 g. Upperparts slate-grey, mottled pale, white stripes over eye, meeting on nape, white breast band. In non-breeding plumage much paler. Female (Plate) a little bigger and more richly coloured than male. Often trusting.

Voice: Soft *'driew driew'* or *'piue piue'*. Courtship song: repeated *'pit pit'*.

Habitat: Arctic tundra, mountain tundra; farmland, steppes on migration.

Food: Insects, spiders, snails, worms.

Breeding: May-Jul, 3 eggs, incubation 25-27 days, young fledge at 26-30 days. Nests in hollow on ground.

1 Turnstone

Arenaria interpres

(Sandpipers and allies)

In Britain: Jan-Dec.

Identification: 23 cm/120 g. Small colourful shorebird, stocky and short-legged; short, pointed bill, sometimes slightly upturned; legs orange-yellow. In non-breeding plumage upperparts dark brown, throat white, dark breast patch. Female a little less colourful than male. In flight appears black-and-white. When running moves head and neck rhythmically back and forth; when searching for food turns over small objects; swims well; on migration mostly in small flocks.

Voice: Soft *'kyug'* (contact call), *'tewke-tewk'*; when agitated *'kikekikekike'*.

Habitat: Rocky coasts, rocky and sandy islands near coast; tundra.

Food: Insects, crustaceans, molluscs.

Breeding: May-Jul, 4 eggs, incubation 22-23 days, young fledge at 19-21 days. Nests on ground.

2 Lapwing

Vanellus vanellus

(Plovers)

In Britain: Jan-Dec.

Identification: 30 cm/200 g. Large wader looking black-and-white at a distance, with long spiky crest; upperparts dark with greenish metallic gloss; face, chin, throat and half-circle breast-band black; belly white, undertail coverts rusty brown. Female with white throat and shorter crest. In non-breeding plumage less richly coloured. In flight broad, rounded, black-and-white wings, in males broader 'hand' (outer wing); tail white with broad black terminal band. Sociable at all times of the year; flight very manoeuvrable with relatively slow, erratic wingbeats; conspicuous courtship display flight of the male with tumbling dives and steep climbs.

Voice: Contact call a disyllabic *'pie-vitt'*; call of male in display flight *'vitt vitt vitt khiuvitt'*.

Habitat: Dried up mud, moors, ploughed fields, meadows, pastures.

Food: Insects, worms, snails.

Breeding: Mar-Jun, 4 eggs, incubation 26-29 days, young fledge at 35-40 days. Nests on ground.

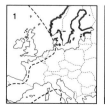

1

2

1 Curlew Sandpiper

Calidris ferruginea

(Sandpipers and allies)

In Britain: Apr-Oct; migrant, does not breed.

Identification: 19 cm/65 g. Dunlin size, but with longer, gently downcurved bill, longer-legged; chestnut with dark spotting, rump white. Female a little paler. In non-breeding plumage similar to Dunlin, but paler, white stripe over eye more obvious. Mostly upright stance.

Voice: 'tirr', 'tirrit'. Trilling song.

Habitat: Arctic tundra, on migration on mudflats.

Food: Worms, leeches, small snails and mussels.

Breeding: Jun-Jul, 4 eggs. Nests in scrape on ground.

2/3 Dunlin

Calidris alpina

(Sandpipers and allies)

In Britain: Jan-Dec.

Identification: 17-19 cm/45-65 g. Commonest small wader; long bill, somewhat downcurved towards tip; upperparts brown-black marked with rufous, underparts with large black belly patch (Plate 2). In non-breeding plumage (Plate 3) upperparts brown-grey, underparts dirty white. Sexes similar. Very sociable; when feeding probes feverishly in mud; flocks fly in tight formation.

Voice: A squeezed 'treerr'. Trilling song.

Habitat: Arctic tundra, coastal meadows, marshes; on migration mainly mudflats.

Food: Insects, small molluscs, lugworms.

Breeding: Apr-Jul, 4 eggs, incubation 20-22 days, young fledge at 19-22 days. Nest hidden in ground vegetation.

4 Little Stint

Calidris minuta

(Sandpipers and allies)

In Britain: Apr-Oct; migrant, does not breed.

Identification: 13 cm/25 g. Barely sparrow-sized sandpiper with relatively short straight bill; upperparts mottled rufous and black, in non-breeding plumage grey; underparts white. Sexes similar. Young with distinct whitish 'V' on back. Associates commonly with Dunlins, similarly feverish when feeding.

Voice: High trembling 'tirtirrtirrit'; flight call 'kip'. Song a rising and falling trill.

Habitat: Wet tundra marshes; on migration open mudflats.

Food: Insects, worms, small molluscs and crustaceans.

Breeding: Jun-Jul, 4 eggs. Nests in scrape on ground.

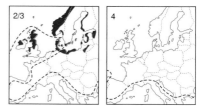

1 Temminck's Stint
Calidris temminckii

(Sandpipers and allies)

In Britain: May-Sep; scarce migrant, rare breeder.

Identification: 14 cm/25 g. Very similar to Little Stint (p. 102), but more elongated, shorter yellowish-green legs, slender bill; plumage greyer, upperparts less mottled. Non-breeding plumage paler than breeding dress. Sexes similar. Flies up high in zigzags to escape from danger (towering); not sociable.

Voice: Soft *'kililili'*, trilling *'tirr'*. Song a cheeping trill.

Habitat: Dwarf scrub tundra, bare plateaus; on migration muddy areas with plenty of cover. *Food:* Insects, snails, worms.

Breeding: May-Jul, 4 eggs, incubation 21-22 days, young fledge at 16-18 days. Nests in scrape on ground.

2 Sanderling
Calidris alba

(Sandpipers and allies)

In Britain: Jan-Dec; does not breed.

Identification: 20 cm/55 g. A little larger and stockier than Dunlin (p. 102), with short straight bill; upperparts in breeding dress marked with rufous, in non-breeding plumage pale grey with blackish patch at shoulder; underparts always pure white (though with chestnut breast when breeding). Sexes similar. In flight broad white wingbar. Sociable; runs rapidly, crouched, after the retreating waves.

Voice: Short *'plit'* or *'tvik'*. Song a purring trill.

Habitat: Arctic tundra; on migration mudflats, especially the open shore along the tideline. *Food:* Insects, molluscs, crustaceans.

Breeding: Jun-Jul, 4 eggs, incubation 24-27 days. Nests in scrape on ground.

3 Knot
Calidris canutus

(Sandpipers and allies)

In Britain: Jan-Dec; does not breed.

Identification: 25 cm/150 g. Large plump sandpiper with short neck, relatively short bill and short legs; upperparts spotted rufous, underparts rusty red. In juvenile plumage (Plate) upperparts ash-grey with white feather edges, underparts yellowish-white. Sexes similar. Very sociable; like Dunlin performs flight acrobatics in tightly bunched flocks.

Voice: Flight call *'tuit-vit'*, *'giug'*. Song recalls Curlew (p. 114).

Habitat: When breeding, on tundra, bare plateaus, otherwise mudflats.

Food: Insects (larvae), spiders, mussels, crustaceans.

Breeding: Jun-Jul, 4 eggs. Nests in scrape on ground.

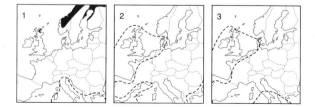

1 Purple Sandpiper

Calidris maritima

(Sandpipers and allies)

In Britain: Aug-May; has bred.

Identification: 21 cm/80 g. A little bigger than Dunlin (p. 102), appears stocky because of its short legs; legs and usually base of bill yellowish; upperparts dark brown, marked rufous and white. Non-breeding plumage (Plate) chiefly brown-grey, belly white. Sexes similar. Looks very dark in flight. Not shy; sociable when not breeding; song flight of male whirring and gliding, often on depressed wings.

Voice: Rather silent when not breeding; when taking flight *'veet'*, *'veet-vit'*, *'tritt-tritt'*. Territorial song fluting and trilling, likened to Green Woodpecker.

Habitat: Tundra, uplands, rocky coastal islands; outside the breeding season in wave-splash zone on rocky coasts.

Food: Small molluscs and crustaceans.

Breeding: Jun-Jul, 4 eggs, incubation 21-22 days, young fledge at 3-4 weeks. Nests in scrape on ground.

Similar species: **Broad-billed Sandpiper** *Limicola falcinellus*. Small sandpiper with long bill, slightly decurved at tip, short legs; upperparts with Snipe-like pattern. Breeds in Scandinavian marshes. Rare visitor to western Europe.

2/3 Red-necked Phalarope

Phalaropus lobatus

(Sandpipers and allies)

In Britain: May-Oct; rare breeder.

Identification: 18 cm/35 g. Very fine black bill; grey lobes of skin on toes; throat white; head of male rufous, of female blackish, the latter altogether more richly coloured than the male (Plate 2, male left, female right). In juvenile plumage (Plate 3) both sexes have upperparts dark slate-grey, with dark eye-stripe, underparts whitish. In flight conspicuous white wingbar. When swimming sits very high on the water, spinning on the spot, nodding head; rarely on land; fast skilful flier.

Voice: In flight *'bitt'*, *'vitt vitt'*; contact call *'vediu vediu'*.

Habitat: Small tundra pools; outside the breeding season mainly the open ocean.

Food: Insects, small crustaceans, spiders, invertebrates.

Breeding: Jun-Jul, 4 eggs, incubation 17-19 days, young fledge at 18-20 days. Nests on ground.

Red-necked Phalarope in flight

1   Redshank   *Tringa totanus*

(Sandpipers and allies)

In Britain: Jan-Dec.

Identification: 28 cm/130 g. Medium-sized wader with long, bright orange-red legs; bill black with red base; upperparts grey-brown, spotted darker, underparts dirty white spotted dark brown; tail barred black-and-white. Non-breeding plumage paler and less spotted. Sexes similar. In flight broad white trailing edge to wing, rump and lower back white. Often perches on fence posts and other raised lookouts; conspicuous display flight of male with winnowing wingbeats.

Voice: Melodious piping *'diu-u'* or *'diu-u-u'*, piercing *'gyib gyib'*. Yodelling song.

Habitat: Wet meadows, moorland, brackish lakes, marshes; outside the breeding season mostly coastal flats.

Food: Insects, earthworms, small frogs, tadpoles.

Breeding: Apr-Jun, 4 eggs, incubation 22-25 days, young fledge from 25 days. Nests on ground.

Similar species: **Terek Sandpiper** *Xenus cinereus*. Smaller than Redshank, bill almost twice length of head, distinctly upcurved. Breeds in northeast Europe.

Marsh Sandpiper *Tringa stagnatilis*. Smaller than Redshank, plumage much paler; long fine pointed bill. On migration occasional in western Europe.

2   Spotted Redshank   *Tringa erythropus*

(Sandpipers and allies)

In Britain: Jan-Dec, but mainly on passage; does not breed.

Identification: 30 cm/150 g. A little bigger than Redshank, more slender-looking because of its longer legs and longer thin bill; legs dark red; plumage grey-black with fine white spotting on upperparts. In non-breeding plumage upperparts ash-grey, spotted white, underparts pale grey; altogether paler than Redshank (Plate: juvenile plumage). Sexes similar. In flight lacks obvious white in wing. When feeding often wades up to belly; swims more readily than other 'shanks, even lands on water.

Voice: Disyllabic *'diu-it'*; when disturbed *'tyicktyicktyick'*. Tuneful rolling song.

Habitat: Wet tundra, moorland at northern edge of the taiga; outside the breeding season on inland waters, coastal bays.

Food: Aquatic insects, small crustaceans, worms, tadpoles, small fish.

Breeding: May-Jul, 4 eggs. Nests in scrape on ground.

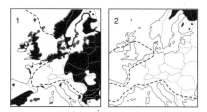

1 ## Greenshank

Tringa nebularia

(Sandpipers and allies)

In Britain: Jan-Dec.

Identification: 31 cm/200 g. Large pale wader with long greenish legs; bill long, slightly upturned; upperparts grey-brown, head and neck finely streaked darker. Non-breeding plumage paler. Sexes similar. Not very sociable; wary.

Voice: Loud ringing *'kyuukyuukyuu'*; song flight of male a piping *'tiu-i'*.

Habitat: Moorland, heaths, lichen-covered uplands close to water; on migration along rivers and lakes, coastal flats.

Food: Worms, crustaceans, aquatic insects, fish.

Breeding: May-Jul, 4 eggs, incubation 23-25 days, young fledge at 28-30 days. Nests in scrape on ground.

2 ## Wood Sandpiper

Tringa glareola

(Sandpipers and allies)

In Britain: Apr-Sep; migrant, rare breeder.

Identification: 20 cm/65 g. Smaller than Redshank (p. 108), shorter, dark bill, legs yellowish-green; upperparts dark grey-brown with small white densely scattered spots; pale stripe over eye. Sexes similar.

Voice: When taking flight a high *'giff giff giff'*. Song performed by both sexes (also given in song flight), recalling Woodlark phrases.

Habitat: Upland bogs, wet heaths, flooded conifer forest; outside the breeding season freshwater margins.

Food: Insects, crustaceans, small snails.

Breeding: May-Jul, 4 eggs, incubation 22-23 days, young fledge at about 4 weeks. Nests among scrub or in old thrush nest.

3 ## Green Sandpiper

Tringa ochropus

(Sandpipers and allies)

In Britain: Jan-May, Jul-Dec.

Identification: 23 cm/80 g. Similar to Wood Sandpiper, but upperparts dark brown, densely spotted paler; in non-breeding plumage upperparts brownish-grey, spotting less noticeable; underparts white. In flight snow-white rump contrasts strongly with dark wings. Usually solitary; when flushed flies off high, calling, weaving erratically.

Voice: Sharp high *'tlui-titit'*.

Habitat: Wooded bogs; on migration lakes and ditches with good cover.

Food: Insects, spiders, worms.

Breeding: Apr-Jun, 4 eggs, incubation 20-23 days, young fledge at about 4 weeks. Nests in old thrush nest.

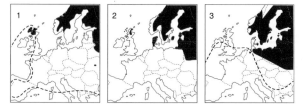

1

2

3

Common Sandpiper
Actitis hypoleucos

(Sandpipers and allies)

In Britain: Apr-Oct.

Identification: 20 cm/55 g. Small, short-legged and short-billed wader; upperparts olive-brown, finely spotted, neck and sides of breast grey-brown, sharply contrasted with white underparts; legs greenish. Sexes similar. In flight striking white wingbar, tail olive-brown above with white sides. Teeters hind part of body almost constantly, bobs head; when flushed flies low over the water, alternating rapid, shallow wingbeats and glides on gently bowed wings; often perches on stones and washed up wood close to water; song flight of male with winnowing wingbeats on zigzag course.

Voice: Ringing *'hihdidihihdidi'*, the first syllable emphasised and higher-pitched; when disturbed a long *'iit'*. Song of male *'titihihihi'*.

Habitat: Vegetated gravel and sand banks along rivers and lakes; on migration also ditches and small water-bodies, concrete banks and harbours.

Food: Insects, spiders, small crustaceans.

Breeding: May-Jul, 4 eggs, incubation 21-22 days, young able to fly from about 20 days. Nest well hidden on ground.

Ruff
Philomachus pugnax

(Sandpipers and allies)

In Britain: Jan-Dec; rarely breeds.

Identification: Male 29 cm/170 g; female 23 cm/100 g. Male in breeding plumage (Plate 2) with conspicuous 'ear tufts' and huge neck ruff; colour of head and ruff very variable from almost black through chestnut to white; face bare; legs always pale. Female (Plate 3) considerably smaller, lacking head and neck adornments, upperparts grey-brown, pale feather fringes giving scaly appearance. In non-breeding plumage male like female. Conspicuous lek-display of males with mock-fighting.

Voice: Almost silent; in flight occasionally *'kriu'*.

Habitat: Damp meadows with short grass, wet bogs and heaths, dunes, dwarf scrub tundra; on migration mudflats.

Food: Insects, small crustaceans, molluscs, worms.

Breeding: May-Jul, 4 eggs, incubation 20-22 days, young fledge at 25 days. Nests on ground.

non-breeding plumage

♂

Ruff

lekking bird

1 Curlew

Numenius arquata

(Sandpipers and allies)

In Britain: Jan-Dec.

Identification: 53-58 cm/600-900 g. Very large wader with long downcurved bill. Upperparts brownish-grey, thickly mottled black-brown; underparts paler with less dense markings; legs grey-green, female with longer bill, more strongly curved in outer third. In flight conspicuous white rump patch extending up back, tail narrowly barred. Flight quick with relatively slow wingbeats; flocks often fly in V-formation or in line; wary.

Voice: Very musical, whistling; flight call a deep, rising *'dliui', 'kleui'*. Display song of male given in flight, a loud rising accelerating series of *'gui'* notes, ending in a trill.

Habitat: Extensive, open damp meadows, moorland, grassland, marshes; outside the breeding season mostly mudflats, flooded fields, muddy river and lake shores.

Food: Insects and their larvae, spiders, small crustaceans, molluscs, worms; in autumn also berries.

Breeding: Apr-Jul, 4 eggs, incubation 27-29 days, young fledge at 5 weeks. Nests on ground in low vegetation.

2 Whimbrel

Numenius phaeopus

(Sandpipers and allies)

In Britain: Apr-Sep.

Identification: 41 cm/500 g. Smaller than Curlew, shorter somewhat thicker and less decurved bill; upperparts darker, mottled pale, conspicuous dark brown crown stripes. Sexes similar. On breeding grounds perches on bushes and trees; sociable, often in company of Curlews.

Voice: Unmusical laughing *'ki-iiiiii'* or *'bibibibibi', 'diuyuyuyuyu'*. Song of male *'uid-uid-uid'*.

Habitat: Uncultivated marshes and heaths, tundra; outside the breeding season flat sandy and muddy coasts, small pools near coast, also rocky shores.

Food: Insects, snails, worms, crustaceans; in autumn mostly crowberries and bilberries.

Breeding: May-Jul, 4 eggs, incubation 27-28 days, young fledge at 5-6 weeks. Nests on ground.

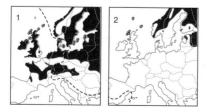

1 Black-tailed Godwit

Limosa limosa

(Sandpipers and allies)

In Britain: Jan-Dec.

Identification: 41 cm/300 g. Large wader with long legs and very long straight, or very slightly upcurved, orange-yellow or pink bill, black in outer third; upperparts brown-grey with black spotting, head, neck and breast rusty brown, belly white with strong blackish cross-barring. Female less intensely coloured, often almost grey. In non-breeding plumage grey-brown with unbarred white belly.

In flight striking broad white wingbar and white tail with broad black terminal band; legs extend well beyond tail. When not breeding very sociable, often with other waders and ducks, often wades up to belly when feeding; in spring conspicuous display flight of male with slow wingbeats, diving and climbing steeply as well as circling erratically.

Voice: Call *'dididi'*, *'diit'*, *'gritta gritta gritta'*; in high song flight characteristic *'grutte grutte'*.

Habitat: Grassy damp meadows, unimproved grassland, flat coastal pastures.

Food: Earthworms, grasshoppers, beetles, snails, small crustaceans, tadpoles.

Breeding: Apr-Jun, 4 eggs, incubation 22-24 days, young fledge at 28-35 days. Nests on ground.

2 Bar-tailed Godwit

Limosa lapponica

(Sandpipers and allies)

In Britain: Jan-Dec; does not breed.

Identification: 38 cm/300 g. Similar to Black-tailed Godwit, but rather smaller, with shorter weakly upturned bill; upperparts red-brown, marked black, underparts unbarred rusty red. Female a little larger than male, with longer bill, less richly coloured. In juvenile plumage (Plate) upperparts grey-brown strongly marked, underparts whitish. In flight lacks white wingbar. Outside the breeding season sociable, often with Curlews, Black-tailed Godwits, Oystercatchers; flocks migrate in slanting lines.

Voice: Flight call a nasal *'ved ved ved'*, *'gegegege'*. Yodelling song given by male in flight.

Habitat: Marshy tundra, dwarf scrub taiga with pools; outside the breeding season mainly on fine muddy shores.

Food: Lugworms, small mussels, snails and crustaceans, insect larvae, beetles.

Breeding: May-Jun, 3-4 eggs, incubation 20-21 days. Nests on ground.

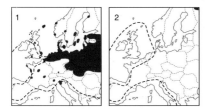

116

1 Woodcock

Scolopax rusticola

(Sandpipers and allies)

In Britain: Jan-Dec.

Identification: 34 cm/300 g. Large chunky snipe with long stout bill; large eyes, high up on head; plumage colour of bark, with 3-4 broad dark cross bands on head. Sexes similar. In flight appears thickset and neckless, wings broad and rounded. Solitary, mostly crepuscular; when flushed zigzags up, soon dropping again; slow display flight (roding) at tree canopy height.

Voice: Male in display flight utters *'uorrt uorrt'*, *'psiwick'*.

Habitat: Damp deciduous and mixed woodland.

Food: Earthworms, insects, spiders.

Breeding: Mar-Jul, 4 eggs, incubation 20-24 days, young fledge at 20 days. Nest well camouflaged on ground.

2 Jack Snipe

Lymnocryptes minimus

(Sandpipers and allies)

In Britain: Sep-Apr.

Identification: 19 cm/60 g. Very small, relatively short-billed snipe; upperparts with weak greenish metallic gloss, two cream-coloured stripes. In flight tail lacking white. When flushed lands again within 50 m.

Voice: Rather silent; noise made in display flight (by both sexes) sounds like cantering.

Habitat: Marshes, silted up areas, wooded bogs; wet meadows, flooded land.

Food: Worms, snails, insects.

Breeding: May-Jul, 4 eggs, incubation 22-24 days. Nests on ground.

3 Snipe

Gallinago gallinago

(Sandpipers and allies)

In Britain: Jan-Dec.

Identification: 27 cm/110 g. Very long-billed, short-legged snipe; plumage cryptic, upperparts brownish with black markings and whitish stripes. Sexes similar. When flushed climbs away in zigzags (towering); remains well hidden; territorial flight of male with bleating *'vvv'* noise made by vibration of outer tail feathers.

Voice: When flushed *'itsch'*. Display song of male and female: *'tiucke tiucke tiucke'*, given from ground.

Habitat: Marshes, silted up areas.

Food: Worms, crustaceans, snails, insects.

Breeding: Mar-Jul, 4 eggs, incubation 18-20 days, young fly at 19-20 days. Nests on ground.

1 Stone-curlew

Burhinus oedicnemus

(Stone-curlews)

In Britain: Mar-Oct, uncommon.

Identification: 41 cm/450 g. Large stocky wader with large head, large yellow eyes and powerful bill, yellow in basal half; powerful, long yellow legs; plumage of upperparts pale brown with black-brown and whitish streaking, pale horizontal wingbars. Sexes similar. In flight two white wingbars visible. Mainly active at dusk; by day rests sitting on haunches in cryptic posture; very sensitive to disturbance.

Voice: Far-carrying harsh *'kreew-li'* recalling Curlew (p. 114); often several individuals call at the same time.

Habitat: Dry, sandy and stony areas with sparse vegetation, stony fields, large clearings in dry heathy pine woods.

Food: Worms, snails, grasshoppers, frogs, reptiles, young birds, small mammals.

Breeding: Apr-Aug, 2 eggs, incubation 25-27 days, young fledge at 35-40 days; 1-2 broods per year. Nests on ground.

2 Collared Pratincole

Glareola pratincola

(Pratincoles)

In Britain: Rare vagrant.

Identification: 25 cm/85 g. Tern-like wader with short, somewhat downcurved bill, red at base, and short legs; upperparts olive-brown; chin and throat creamy-buff, with black surround; lores black, in female (Plate) brownish. In non-breeding plumage throat with dark markings, back feathers with pale fringes. In flight long pointed wings; black, deeply forked tail, held closed in a point; underwing rufous. Sociable; hawks for flying insects mainly in morning and evening, constantly calling.

Voice: When breeding *'karya karya'*, *'git git git'*, *'pirye pirye'*.

Habitat: Steppes and salt flats, dry meadows, fallow fields; usually close to water.

Food: Grasshoppers, beetles, moths.

Breeding: May-Jul, 3 eggs, incubation 17-18 days, young fly at 30 days. Colonial breeder; nests on ground.

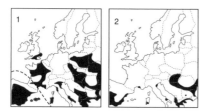

1   Great Skua   *Stercorarius skua*
(Skuas)

In Britain: Mar-Nov.

Identification: 58 cm/1.4 kg. A little larger and considerably stockier than Herring Gull (p. 130); short slightly wedge-shaped tail, bill black, hooked at tip; plumage dark brown. Female a little bigger than male. In flight very broad rounded wings, short tail, conspicuous pale wing flash. Very aggressive, chases other seabirds to steal their prey.

Voice: Barking *'ok ok ok'*, shrill *'skirr'*, whimpering *'a-ekh'*.

Habitat: Marshes and moorland near to coast, islands with tundra vegetation; outside the breeding season the open ocean and coasts.

Food: Stolen prey; eggs and young of other seabirds.

Breeding: May-Jul, 2 eggs, incubation 28-30 days, young independent at 6-7 weeks. Nests on ground.

2   Arctic Skua   *Stercorarius parasiticus*
(Skuas)

In Britain: Apr-Oct.

Identification: 46 cm/400 g. Common Gull-sized with two short pointed tail projections; dark morph predominantly dark brown; pale morph (Plate) with whitish underparts, cheeks and neck yellowish. In flight recalls falcon, with long, narrow pointed wings; very rapid and agile; chases other seabirds for their prey.

Voice: High-pitched hoarse *'ihehr'*, howling *'ka-ouh'*.

Habitat: Moorland, damp heaths close to coast, flat islands, tundra; outside the breeding season mainly the open ocean.

Food: Robs seabirds; fish, small rodents, birds' eggs.

Breeding: May-Jul, 2 eggs, incubation 24-28 days, young fledge at about 1 month. Nests on ground.

3   Long-tailed Skua   *Stercorarius longicaudus*
(Skuas)

In Britain: May-Jun, Sep-Oct.

Identification: 51-56 cm/280 g. Size of Black-headed Gull, with long pointed tail extension, up to 25 cm long. In flight appears graceful and tern-like, with long narrow wings, long tail streamers. Often hovers.

Voice: When breeding a screeching *'kri kri'*.

Habitat: Tundra, moorland; outside the breeding season the open ocean.

Food: Lemmings, small birds; robs seabirds.

Breeding: May-Jul, 2 eggs, incubation 23 days, young independent at 3-4 weeks. Nests on ground.

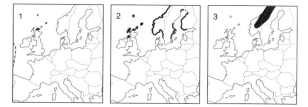

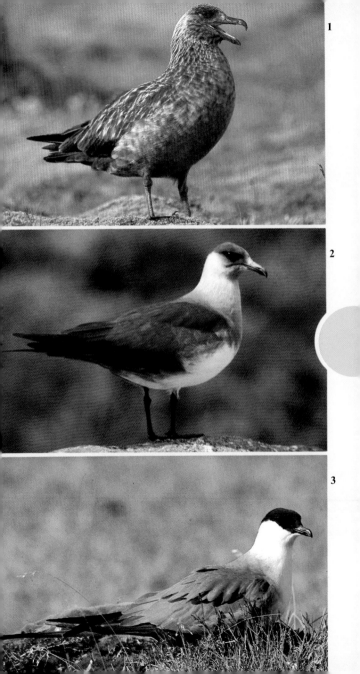

1

2

3

Black-headed Gull
Larus ridibundus

(Gulls)

In Britain: Jan.-Dec.

Identification: 35-38 cm/230-260 g. Commonest gull inland; slender dark red bill, red legs; in breeding plumage (Plate 1) head, chin and throat chocolate brown, upperparts pale grey, rest of plumage white. In non-breeding plumage (Plate 2) white head with dark mark on ear-coverts. Sexes similar. Young with upperparts marked brownish, black tail band.

Flight: Tips of primaries black, leading edge of wing white. At all seasons sociable; often on rubbish tips; in winter common on urban waters.

Voice: Commonly *'kveer'*, *'krrriya'*, *'arrererr'*, *'gegegeg'* and other screeching noises; especially vocal when breeding.

Habitat: Water-bodies with silted up areas, bogs, marshes, sand- and gravel-banks; outside the breeding season inland waters and sea coasts.

Food: Varied; beetles, dragonflies, snails, worms, fish, carrion, waste.

Breeding: Apr-Jul, 3 eggs, incubation 22-24 days, young fledge at 5-6 weeks. Colonial breeder; nest of vegetation, such as old reeds.

first-winter plumage

Little Gull
Larus minutus

(Gulls)

In Britain: Jan.-Dec.; does not breed.

Identification: 28 cm/120 g. Similar to Black-headed Gull, but much smaller; black (not brown) head, upperwing pale grey with no black; short red legs. In winter plumage dark ear-spot, top of head with faded dark patch. Sexes similar. Underwing blackish. Young as winter adult but upperparts brownish. Young with blackish 'W' across upperwing, black tip to tail. Flight tern-like, light and elegant; often in company with Black-headed Gulls or Black Terns.

Voice: Tern-like hard *'kyeck'*, *'gyiig'*, *'kik-ki-ki'*.

Habitat: Well vegetated inland lakes with stands of sedge, horsetail and reeds, sparsely overgrown lakes, coastal bays; outside the breeding season mainly sea coasts and the open sea, also inland lakes.

Food: Flying insects, aquatic insects, small fish, invertebrates, worms, crustaceans.

Breeding: May-Jun, 2-3 eggs, incubation 23-25 days, young fledge at 21-24 days. Colonial breeder; nests on dry ground in marshes.

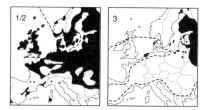

1

2

3

1 · Mediterranean Gull — *Larus melanocephalus*
(Gulls)

In Britain: Jan-Dec; increasing.

Identification: 36-38 cm/200-350 g. Very pale with black hood, white eye-crescents; back pale blue-grey; legs rather long, drooping bill red. Young rather like young Common Gull in plumage-pattern.

Voice: In display a repeated *'whaa'*; also *'kee-ow'*; alarm call *'ga-ga-ga-ga'*.

Habitat: Marshes, coastal lowlands; outside breeding season along coasts.

Food: Insects, crustaceans, small fish, scraps.

Breeding: May-Jul, 3 eggs, incubation 23-25 days, young fledge at 35-40 days. Nests on ground, in colonies.

2 · Glaucous Gull — *Larus hyperboreus*
(Gulls)

In Britain: Oct-Mar.

Identification: 62-68 cm/1.2-2 kg. Very large, fierce, pale gull. Young birds creamy-buff looking very pale in flight, pink bill with black tip. Adults pale grey above, otherwise all white, including wing-tips.

Voice: Similar to Herring Gull.

Habitat: Arctic coasts; in winter fishing harbours, reservoirs, waste-tips.

Food: Fish, small mammals, carrion, birds' eggs, scraps.

Breeding: May-Jul, 3 eggs, incubation 27-28 days, young fledge at 45-50 days.

3 · Iceland Gull — *Larus glaucoides*
(Gulls)

In Britain: Nov-Apr.

Identification: 52-60 cm/730-860 g. Plumage sequences very similar to Glaucous Gull. Smaller, with more gentle expression, relatively longer- and narrower-winged.

Voice: Higher-pitched than Herring Gull.

Habitat: As Glaucous Gull.

Food: Mainly fish, also eggs, carrion.

Breeding: May-Jul, 2-3 eggs, incubation and fledging periods not known.

1 Great Black-backed Gull
Larus marinus

(Gulls)

In Britain: Jan-Dec.

Identification: 64-79 cm/1.6-1.9 kg. Very large gull with flesh-coloured legs; back and upperwing sooty black, rest of plumage, including trailing edge and outermost tips of wings white; bill yellow, very powerful. Outside breeding season head streaked grey. Female smaller than male, with weaker bill. Young very similar to young Herring Gull (p. 130), but with greater plumage contrast, head and underparts paler, not assuming adult plumage until three and a half years old. Majestic in flight, with much gliding; not as sociable as Herring Gull; common at fish docks; follows fishing boats.

Voice: Flight call *'krau'*; hoarse, laughing, commonly repeated *'ouk'*, muffled *'gog'*; when disturbed a deep *'ga-ag-ag-ag'*.

Habitat: Small rocky islands, rocky and shingle coasts, coastal marshes and heaths; outside the breeding season all types of coast; waste tips.

Food: Eggs and young of shorebirds and seabirds, carrion, waste.

Breeding: Apr-Jul, 2-3 eggs, incubation 26-30 days, young fledge at 7-8 weeks. Large nest on ground.

first-winter plumage

2 Lesser Black-backed Gull
Larus fuscus

(Gulls)

In Britain: Jan-Dec.

Identification: 52-56 cm/800-1100 g. Similar to Herring Gull (p. 130), but upperwing and back dark grey to blackish, depending on race; legs yellow, in winter mostly duller. Female mostly smaller than male. Young in first winter hard to distinguish from young Herring Gull, in second winter upperparts clearly darker.

Voice: Similar to Great Black-backed Gull, a hoarse *'ouk ouk'*, but somewhat higher; when threatened a nasal *'au'*, *'gagaga'*.

Habitat: Sandy and rocky beaches, bogs, dwarf scrub, coastal grassland; large rivers, islands in freshwater and brackish lakes; outside the breeding season the open sea, islands and rocky coasts; waste tips.

Food: Fish, mussels, crustaceans, insects, mice, carrion, waste.

Breeding: May-Jul, 3 eggs, incubation 25-27 days, young fledge at 5-6 weeks. Colonial breeder; untidy, large nest on ground.

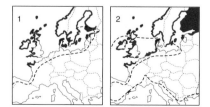

1   Herring Gull

Larus argentatus

(Gulls)

In Britain: Jan-Dec.

Identification: 56-66 cm/900-1300 g. Commonest large coastal gull; back and wings silvery grey, wing tips black with white mirrors, rest of plumage white; bill yellow with red spot; eyes yellow; legs of the northwest European races flesh-coloured, in some other races yellow. Female usually smaller than male. Young brownish with paler feather fringes, bill black. Very sociable; often on waste tips.

Voice: Howling and miaowing *'kyau'*, often repeated; laughing *'kiya kiya kiya kiyau kiyau'*.

Habitat: All types of coast; waters close to coast, large lakes and rivers.

Food: Fish, small animals, carrion, waste.

Breeding: Apr-Jun, 2-3 eggs, incubation 26-30 days, young fledge at 5-6 weeks. Nests on ground.

2   Common Gull

Larus canus

(Gulls)

In Britain: Jan-Dec.

Identification: 41 cm/360 g. Smaller than Herring Gull; head roundish, bill and legs greenish-yellow, eyes dark. Sexes similar. Young with grey-brown upperparts, broad black terminal tail-band. In winter in small numbers in towns.

Voice: Higher and shriller than Herring Gull *'giya' giya'*; *'e-e-eiie-eiie'*, *'kyau'*.

Habitat: Sea coasts and waters close to coast, inland lakes, fields.

Food: Insects, invertebrates, fish, mice, carrion, waste.

Breeding: May-Jul, 3 eggs, incubation 24-28 days, young fledge at 5 weeks. Nests on ground.

3   Kittiwake

Rissa tridactyla

(Gulls)

In Britain: Jan-Dec.

Identification: 41 cm/440 g. Pure white with grey mantle, uniform black wing-tips, yellow, slender bill, dark eyes, black feet with only three toes. Sexes similar. Young with black-brown bar across nape and black terminal tail band. Very elegant flight; often tern-like dives.

Voice: On breeding grounds penetrating *'kiti-veek'*; harsh *'gag gag'*.

Habitat: When breeding steep cliffs, otherwise mostly the open ocean.

Food: Fish, invertebrates, crustaceans, waste.

Breeding: May-Jul, 2 eggs, incubation 24-28 days, young fledge at 5-8 weeks. Colonial breeder; nests on narrow cliff ledges, also on buildings.

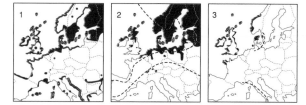

1 Sandwich Tern

Sterna sandvicensis

(Terns)

In Britain: Mar-Oct.

Identification: 41 cm/250 g. Slender black bill with yellow tip, black crest; legs black; in post-breeding plumage (Plate) with white forehead. Sexes similar. Young with scaly brown head and upperparts. Very sociable and noisy; dives for food.

Voice: Loud 'kirrik', 'krick' or 'krikrikri'.

Habitat: Sand or shingle beaches on sea coast, flat rocky coasts.

Food: Small fish, crustaceans, molluscs, worms.

Breeding: May-Jul, 1-2 eggs, incubation 22-26 days, young fledge at about 30 days. Colonial breeder. Nests on ground.

2 Common Tern

Sterna hirundo

(Terns)

In Britain: Apr-Sep.

Identification: 35 cm/130 g. Slender orange-red bill with black tip; legs red; tail does not extend beyond closed wings; in winter white forehead, bill blackish with red base. Sexes similar. Young with white forehead and brownish speckled upperparts. Sociable; flight very elegant; dives for food.

Voice: Piercing 'krierr', 'kirrikirri' and 'kit kit kirr'.

Habitat: Sand and shingle banks of inland waters, flat sea coasts, dunes.

Food: Small fish, crustaceans, tadpoles, aquatic insects.

Breeding: May-Jul, 2-3 eggs, incubation 20-23 days, young fledge at 24-30 days. Colonial breeder. Nests on ground.

3 Arctic Tern

Sterna paradisaea

(Terns)

In Britain: Apr-Oct.

Identification: 35 cm/110 g. Like Common Tern but uniform blood-red bill, shorter legs, darker underparts, tail extending beyond wing tips when at rest; in winter forehead and crown white, bill and legs blackish. Sexes similar. Young similar to young Common Tern. Sociable; flight very elegant; dives for food.

Voice: Call 'kriurr', 'krier' and 'ki ki'.

Habitat: Sand or shingle beaches on sea coast, tundra.

Food: Small fish, crustaceans.

Breeding: May-Jul, 2-3 eggs, incubation 20-22 days, young fledge at 20-30 days. Colonial breeder.

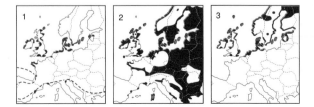

1　Little Tern
Sterna albifrons

(Terns)

In Britain: Apr-Sep.

Identification: 24 cm/50 g. Tiny! Bill yellow with black tip, forehead white, legs orange-yellow; in winter black eyestripe and black rear crown. Sexes similar. Young like winter adults, but upperparts flecked brownish. Less sociable than other terns; hovers frequently; feeds by diving.

Voice: Call *'ved ved'*, *'kitt kitt'* or *'kirri-kirri'*.

Habitat: Sandy or shingle beaches on sea coast, also inland waters.

Food: Small fish, crustaceans, insects.

Breeding: May-Jul, 2-3 eggs, incubation 20-22 days, young fledge at 17-21 days. Breeds on ground in loose colonies, also singly.

2　Black Tern
Chlidonias niger

(Terns)

In Britain: Apr-Oct on migration; does not breed.

Identification: 24 cm/65 g. Small, blackish tern, bill and legs black, wings grey above and below, tail grey. Underwing coverts white; in winter forehead and underparts white, black mark on side of neck. Sexes similar. Young similar to winter adult. Flies low over the water.

Voice: Call *'krierr'*, *'krek'* or *'kik'*.

Habitat: Inland waters with rich plant growth.

Food: Insects, small frogs and fish.

Breeding: May-Jul, 2-3 eggs, incubation 21-22 days, young fledge at 21 days. Breeds in loose colonies on floating vegetation.

3　Whiskered Tern
Chlidonias hybridus

(Terns)

In Britain: Rare visitor.

Identification: 25 cm/90 g. Grey tern with black cap and white cheeks, bill deep red, legs red, underwing and undertail coverts white; in winter forehead and underparts white, nape black, dark eyestripe. Sexes similar. Young similar to winter adult. Often dives.

Voice: Call croaking *'krik'* or *'krt'*.

Habitat: Inland waters with rich plant growth.

Food: Insects, small frogs and fish.

Breeding: May-Jun, 2-4 eggs, incubation 18-22 days, young fledge at 21-23 days. Breeds in loose colonies on floating vegetation.

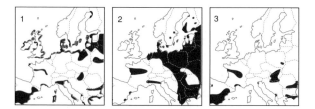

1

2

3

1 Puffin

Fratercula arctica

(Auks)

In Britain: Mar-Aug.

Identification: 30 cm/400 g. Stocky auk with large head and massive, strongly compressed, red-and-yellow striped bill; sides of head white, in winter grey. Sexes similar. Young with grey cheeks and small bill. Sociable; dives a great deal, flight rapid and direct.

Voice: Call a deep *'arrr'* or *'aah'*.

Habitat: Grassy coastal cliffs, not too steep; rocky islands, coastal waters; outside the breeding season the open sea.

Food: Fish (sandeels), crustaceans.

Breeding: Apr-Jul, 1 egg, incubation 35-43 days, young fledge at 40-50 days. Nests in burrows in dense colonies.

2 Black Guillemot

Cepphus grylle

(Auks)

In Britain: Jan-Dec.

Identification: 32 cm/400 g. Black auk with large white wing patches, bill slender and pointed, feet gleaming red; in winter upperparts speckled grey, underparts white. Sexes similar. Young similar to winter adult. Less sociable than other auks; dives regularly.

Voice: Call a high thin *'ssie'*, *'siude-siude'* or *'diusi-diusi'*.

Habitat: Rocky coasts, not too steep, with plenty of crevices, coastal waters, fjords.

Food: Fish, crustaceans, small bottom-living animals.

Breeding: May-Jul, 1-2 eggs, incubation 24-28 days, young fledge at 34-40 days. Nests in small colonies.

3 Little Auk

Alle alle

(Auks)

In Britain: Oct-Mar.

Identification: 20 cm/140 g. Only Starling-sized, with large black head, short, powerful bill and black feet; in winter underparts and cheeks white. Sexes similar. Young similar to winter adult. Sociable; dives often, flight more agile than other auks.

Voice: Call a high vibrating *'trii'*, a whistling *'giff giff'* or chattering *'ga ga garak'*.

Habitat: High cliffs, mountains close to coast, the open sea.

Food: Small planktonic crustaceans.

Breeding: Jun-Jul, 1 egg, incubation 29 days, young fledge at 28 days. Nests in dense colonies in holes in cliffs or earth burrows.

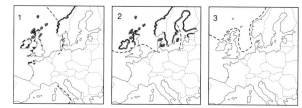

1 Guillemot

Uria aalge

(Auks)

In Britain: Jan-Dec.

Identification: 42 cm/800 g. Slimmer than Razorbill, with slender, pointed, unmarked bill; feet blackish; form with white eyering and narrow white line back to ear coverts ('Bridled Guillemot'); in winter also chin, cheeks and foreneck white, black stripe behind eye. Sexes similar. Young like winter adult. Very sociable, sits in dense groups on rock ledges on the steep breeding cliffs, dives often for long periods, up to two minutes, like all the auks uses half-open wings to swim underwater.

Voice: Call a deep rasping *'arrr'*, *'hadada'*, trilling *'sirrirr'* or miaowing *'yau'*.

Habitat: Steep sea cliffs; outside the breeding season the open sea.

Food: Fish, crustaceans, molluscs.

Breeding: May-Jul, 1 egg, incubation 30-36 days, young leave nest ledge for sea at 18-20 days. Nests in dense colonies.

Similar species: **Brünnich's Guillemot** *Uria lomvia*. Very similar to Guillemot, but shorter thicker bill with narrow white stripe at base. Breeds in Europe only in north Norway, NW Russia, Iceland and Spitzbergen.

2 Razorbill

Alca torda

(Auks)

In Britain: Jan-Dec.

Identification: 40 cm/700 g. Smaller and stockier than Guillemot, deeper, compressed bill with white band and white line from top of bill to eye; in winter also throat, foreneck and sides of neck white. Sexes similar. Young similar to winter adult, bill unmarked. Sociable; dives often for long duration, swims with cocked tail; flight rapid with whirring wings, the tail extending beyond the outstretched feet.

Voice: A deep grating *'orrr'*, *'uorr-orr-or'*.

Habitat: Coastal waters and the open sea; when breeding steep sea cliffs.

Food: Fish, crustaceans, small bottom-living animals.

Breeding: Apr-Jul, 1 egg, incubation 33-36 days, young leave nest ledge for sea at 15-20 days. Nests mostly in small groups amongst colonies of other auks.

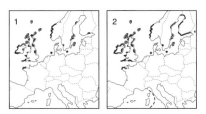

1   Pin-tailed Sandgrouse
Pterocles alchata

(Sandgrouse)

In Britain: Not recorded.

Identification: 37 cm/250 g. Long pointed tail, black eyestripe, belly white. Male with chin and throat black, two narrow black breast bands; female with chin and throat white, three narrow black breast bands, upperparts with wavy bars. In flight the long narrow pointed wings with white undersides and the pointed tail stand out. Flight rapid; flocks fly to water to drink, mostly towards dusk. Wary on the ground, runs like a pigeon.

Voice: Call in flight a nasal *'gang-gang-gang'* and harsh ringing *'grarr ga ga grarr'*.

Habitat: Dry, stony plains, sandy steppes, dried up mudflats.

Food: Seeds, green plant matter.

Breeding: Apr-Jun, 2-3 eggs, incubation 21-23 days, young nidifugous, fly at 3-4 weeks. Nests on ground.

2   Black-bellied Sandgrouse
Pterocles orientalis

(Sandgrouse)

In Britain: Not recorded.

Identification: 34 cm/400 g. Larger and stockier than Pin-tailed Sandgrouse, lacking tail point, belly black. Male with head and upper breast pale grey; female (Plate) with crown and upper breast sandy, finely spotted black. In flight the whitish underwing coverts contrast with the blackish flight feathers and black belly; flight rapid, with soft whistling wing noise; outside breeding season in large flocks, which undertake long flights to water. Wary on the ground.

Voice: Flight call *'djurr-rurr-rurr'*, *'prurrkhiu-prurrkhiu'*, also a whistling *'hee-ye'*.

Habitat: Semi-deserts, steppes, sandy, sparsely vegetated fallow land.

Food: Seeds, green plant material.

Breeding: Apr-Jun, 2-3 eggs, incubation 21-22 days, chicks leave nest after hatching. Nests on ground. The male brings drinking water to the chicks by soaking his belly feathers. He flies to water, often a long way off, wades in up to his belly and allows his feathers to soak up water like a sponge. He then returns to the young, which suck the water greedily from his belly feathers.

1 # Nightjar

Caprimulgus europaeus

(Nightjars)

In Britain: May-Sep.

Identification: 27 cm/65-100 g. Long-tailed, long-winged, large black eyes, small bill, plumage grey-brown, bark-patterned; in flight shows white wing and tail markings. Female lacks white markings. Active at dusk and by night, catches flying insects in agile, silent flight.

Voice: Call *'ak'*, *'kritt-kritt'*; flight call *'kuik'*. Song: an extended purring *'errr-urrr'*; wing-clapping.

Habitat: Open conifer and deciduous woods, heaths.

Food: Flying insects.

Breeding: May-Aug, 2 eggs, incubation 16-21 days, young fledge at 16-18 days; double-brooded. Nests on ground.

2 # Swift

Apus apus

(Swifts)

In Britain: May-Aug.

Identification: 16.5 cm/43 g. Long, sickle-shaped wings, short forked tail, plumage black-brown, throat whitish. Sexes similar. Young with pale feather fringes. Sociable, never on the ground.

Flight: Rapid shallow wingbeats alternate with glides on extended wings.

Voice: Call a loud shrill *'srieh-srieh'*, often in chorus.

Habitat: Villages and towns, cliffs.

Food: Entirely small flying insects.

Breeding: May-Jul, 2-3 eggs, incubation 18-20 days, young fledge at 40-50 days. Once they leave the nest young are completely independent. Nests in colonies under roofs and in crevices in cliffs.

3 # Alpine Swift

Apus melba

(Swifts)

In Britain: Mar-Oct; vagrant.

Identification: 22 cm/100 g. Larger than Swift, altogether paler brown; throat and belly pure white, brown breast band. Sexes similar. Young with pale feather fringes. Sociable, never on the ground; flight like swift, wings often bent further back, faster, but recorded speeds of up to 250 km/h fanciful.

Voice: Long loud trill *'trihihihi'*, falling in pitch.

Habitat: Rocky hills; around very high, mostly isolated buildings.

Food: Entirely small flying insects.

Breeding: May-Aug, 2-3 eggs, incubation 17-23 days, young fledge at 53-66 days. Nests in colonies on steep rock faces; buildings.

Willow Grouse/Red Grouse *Lagopus lagopus*
(Grouse)

In Britain: Jan-Dec.

Identification: 38-41 cm/450-700 g. In summer barred chestnut-brown, wings white, tail black, belly and leg feathering white, red eye wattles; female inconspicuous yellowish-brown with strong barring; in autumn plumage upperparts as in summer, underparts white, brown head; in winter white without black lores, only tail feathers black. Sexes similar.

The **Red Grouse** (map 1 part A) *Lagopus lagopus scoticus* of the British Isles, a race of the Willow Grouse (map 1 part B), is coloured entirely chestnut-brown, winter as well as summer. Presses itself low to ground when danger threatens.

Voice: Call a rapid wooden-sounding '*kvak-kavak-kavak-kvarrr*', short '*gog*', when disturbed at nest '*kui-kui*'.

Habitat: Open taiga, bushy tundra, marshes and moors with willow, birch and dwarf scrub; generally at lower altitudes than Ptarmigan.

Food: Leaves, buds and berries of dwarf shrubs, especially bilberries, cranberries and crowberries; in winter buds and leaves of dwarf birch; in order to get at their food plants, the birds dig long tunnels in the snow. Red Grouse eats mainly heather shoots.

Breeding: Apr-Jun, 6-14 eggs, incubation 21-24 days, young can fly at 2 weeks, long before fully grown. Nests on ground.

Ptarmigan *Lagopus mutus*
(Grouse)

In Britain: Jan-Dec.

Identification: 35 cm/350-510 g. Smaller than Willow Grouse, with weaker bill. In all plumages wings, lower breast, belly and feet white, black lores, red wattles; in summer upperparts, upper breast and flanks finely barred brown-black (Plate 2); female dark brown to yellowish-brown, also breast and belly barred dark. Winter plumage white apart from black lores and tail (Plate 3); female like male, but without the black lores. Conspicuous display flight; in small flocks outside breeding season.

Voice: A wooden rasping '*arr-aka-ga*'; in display '*euviiii-errr*'; contact call of male '*korr*', of female '*kiie*'.

Habitat: Mountain plateaus above the tree-line; high rocky meadows and slopes; tundra.

Food: Leaves and buds of alpine plants, bilberries, cranberries, crowberries and other berries; insects.

Breeding: May-Jul, 4-11 eggs, incubation 23-24 days, young can fly at 10 days, long before fully grown. Nests on ground.

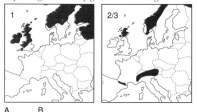

A   B

Capercaillie   *Tetrao urogallus*
(Grouse)

In Britain: Jan-Dec.

Identification: Male 86 cm/4.2 kg; female 62 cm/2 kg. Pronounced sexual differences. Male (Plate 1) dark blue-grey to black with iridescent green breast, wings dark brown with white patch at carpal, bill whitish. Female (Plate 2) similar to greyhen, but larger, with coarser more contrasting barring, rufous breast patch, rounded tail. Flies off noisily, clattering; in winter often in trees. Cocks display alone (also in trees) with strongly fanned tail. Very susceptible to disturbance, especially when breeding.

Voice: Display song of male consists of guttural and grinding-sharpening noises *'go golup golup g'lup g'luppuppupp tschedede schischedede'*; female a Pheasant-like *'guck guck'*, rarely heard.

Habitat: Large mixed and coniferous forests with many dead trees and good bilberry cover.

Food: Weeds, berries, insects (ant pupae important food for young); in winter chiefly conifer shoots.

Breeding: Apr-Jun, 5-12 eggs, incubation 24-26 days, young independent at 3 months. Nests on ground.

Black Grouse   *Tetrao tetrix*
(Grouse)

In Britain: Jan-Dec.

Identification: Male 53 cm/1250 g; female 41 cm/950 g. Pronounced sexual differences. Male (Plate 4) plumage glossy blue-black, with strongly pronounced red wattles over eyes; lyre-shaped forked tail. Female ('greyhen') (Plate 3) cryptically coloured yellowish-brown, barred darker, similar to female Capercaillie but distinctly smaller, lacking rufous on breast, tail shallowly forked, wattles poorly developed. Often sits in trees; lek-display of males on open ground; display posture with strongly fanned tail and gleaming white spread undertail coverts.

Voice: Courtship song of male a far-carrying rolling *'urrurhurrhu urrurhurhu tschuuüsch urrurhurrhu'*; when disturbed *'kri kriao'*; female a nasal cackling.

Habitat: Open moorland and heathland with sparse trees or bushes; upland regions.

Food: Buds of deciduous and coniferous trees, leaves and berries of bilberry, cranberry and crowberry, insects (especially when rearing young).

Breeding: May-Jun, 7-10 eggs, incubation 26-27 days, young independent at 3 months. Nests on ground.

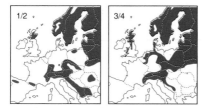

1 Hazel Hen
Bonasa bonasia
(Grouse)

In Britain: Not recorded.
Identification: 36 cm/400 g. Small crest, relatively long tail with black terminal band, upperparts mottled rusty brown (northern race grey), underparts whitish with black markings, black throat-patch bordered white, red wattles. Female lacking black on throat.
Voice: Song of male Goldcrest-like, a high *'tsieh-tsissieh-tititiuit titi'*; alarm call *'vitvitvit'*; female call *'tititi'*.
Habitat: Mixed woodland with rich undergrowth.
Food: Buds of deciduous trees and bushes, berries, insects.
Breeding: Apr-Jun, 7-11 eggs, incubation 23-25 days, young can fly at 2 weeks, not fully grown until 4-6 weeks. Nests on ground.

2 Red-legged Partridge
Alectoris rufa
(Gamebirds)

In Britain: Jan-Dec; introduced.
Identification: 32-34 cm/500 g. Grey-brown upperparts; striking head-pattern of creamy stripe over eye, whitish throat bordered with black, the black extending as broken streaking on to the upper breast, forming a 'necklace'; barred flanks. Red legs. Sexes similar.
Voice: A harsh repeated *'chuk chuk chuk-ar'*.
Habitat: Farmland with hedgerows, open dry countryside, vineyards.
Food: Mainly vegetable matter, seeds; also some insects in summer.
Breeding: May-Jun, 10-16 eggs, incubation 23-24 days, young can flutter at 10 days, become full-size in 50-60 days. Nests on ground.

3 Grey Partridge
Perdix perdix
(Gamebirds)

In Britain: Jan-Dec.
Identification: 30 cm/380 g. Face and throat brick-red, underparts pale grey, dark brown horseshoe-shaped belly patch, wings marked with red-brown, short and rounded. Tail short, showing reddish in flight. In female shoulders and upperwing coverts mottled yellowish, belly patch smaller. Loud wing noise when taking off; in winter in larger groups.
Voice: A hoarse *'kirreck'*, when flushed *'pitt pitt'* or *'rep rep'*.
Habitat: Agricultural landscape of small fields, copses and hedges.
Food: Grass, clover, weeds, seeds, insects.
Breeding: Apr-Jun, 10-20 eggs, incubation 25 days, young can fly at 13-14 days, before fully grown. Nests on ground.

1 Quail

Coturnix coturnix

(Gamebirds)

In Britain: May-Sep; uncommon.

Identification: 18 cm/100 g. Smallest European gamebird, dumpy, extremely short-tailed, long, pointed wings. Upperparts brownish with pale and dark striping, cream-coloured stripe over eye, underparts cream-coloured, chin and throat black; female (Plate) with chin and throat whitish, breast spotted. Remains hidden, escapes mostly on foot; the only migrant amongst the gamebirds.

Voice: Repeated, far-carrying *'pick-per-vick'*, the first note preceded by a soft hissing *'khau-vah'*; female *'quip-ip'* often synchronised with the last two syllables of the male's song.

Habitat: Steppes, open farmland, fields, especially with cereals and clover; meadows.

Food: Insects, spiders, worms, snails; shoots, buds and seeds of weeds and cereals.

Breeding: Apr-Jul, 7-14 eggs, incubation 18-19 days, young can flutter at 11, fly well at 19 days. Nests on ground.

2/3 Pheasant

Phasianus colchicus

(Gamebirds)

In Britain: Jan-Dec.

Identification: Male 66-89 cm/1.2 kg; female 53-63 cm/1 kg.
Chicken-sized gamebird with very long pointed tail. Male (Plate 2) with crown and neck dark iridescent green, red wattles around the eyes, small feather 'ears', mostly a white neck ring; remainder of plumage coppery-red, with black scaly markings, tail feathers with black barring; female (Plate 3) with protective colours of yellow-brown, marked black, tail shorter. Flight rapid and direct; in winter in flocks. The Pheasant was introduced from Asia to Europe for hunting. Many Pheasants are reared and released annually for shooting.

Voice: Territorial call of male a loud squawking *'kukuk'*, followed by a clattering whirring of wings; when taking off *'gugugug'*; female when flushed *'tsik tsik'* as well as a cackling noise.

Habitat: Varied farmland with fields bordering woodland and copses.

Food: Green plant matter, cereals, crops, seeds, berries, insects and worms.

Breeding: Apr-Jun, 8-12 eggs, incubation 23-24 days, the hen alone caring for the young; young can fly at 10-12 days, long before fully grown. Nests on ground.

Turtle Dove

Streptopelia turtur

(Pigeons and doves)

In Britain: Apr-Sep.

Identification: 27 cm/150 g. Smallest European dove, very slim, with black-and-white striped patch on side of neck; wing-covert feathers blackish with rufous fringes; tail graduated with white terminal band. Sexes similar, but female a little paler. Flight rapid and dashing, without noticeable wing noise. Timid.

Voice: Repeated purring *'turrr'*.

Habitat: Farmland, copses, open woodland, parkland.

Food: Mainly seeds and green plant material.

Breeding: May-Aug, 2 eggs, incubation 13-16 days, young fledge at 18-23 days; double-brooded. Tree-nester.

Collared Dove

Streptopelia decaocto

(Pigeons and doves)

In Britain: Jan-Dec.

Identification: 32 cm/200 g. Small, very pale dove with black neck collar and reddish eyes, basal half of tail black. Sexes similar. Flight dashing with musical wing noise; conspicuous territorial and display flight. Associates with man, not shy.

Voice: Repeated, monotonous *'gu-guh-gu'*.

Habitat: Villages and towns, gardens and parks.

Food: Mainly grain; visits bird feeders in winter.

Breeding: Mar-Oct, 2 eggs, incubation 14-18 days, young fledge at 16-19 days; 2-3 broods a year. Nests mostly in trees.

Stock Dove

Columba oenas

(Pigeons and doves)

In Britain: Jan-Dec.

Identification: 33 cm/300 g. More slender than Rock Dove, lacking white in plumage, eyes dark, sides of neck metallic green. Female upperparts with brownish tone. Whistling wing noise; circling display flight.

Voice: Territorial song *'bu-hu-u-up'*, *'hu-ru-u'* or *'hu-ve'*; when disturbed *'ru'*.

Habitat: Thinned woodland with stands of old trees, parkland; dunes and rocky coasts.

Food: Chiefly seeds, berries and green plant material.

Breeding: Mar-Sep, 2 eggs, incubation 16-18 days, young fledge at 23-28 days; 2-3 broods a year. Nests in holes, often old woodpecker holes; also uses nestboxes.

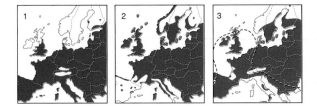

1

2

3

1 Woodpigeon *Columba palumbus*

(Pigeons and doves)

In Britain: Jan-Dec.

Identification: 41 cm/500 g. Larger and longer-tailed than Rock Dove, with conspicuous white patches on sides of neck, throat and breast vinous red, eyes pale yellow; in flight white band across wing obvious. Female with smaller neck patch. Wary; often on farmland; whistling wing noise, display flight.

Voice: Muffled cooing *'ruguhgu gugu'*, stressed on the second syllable.

Habitat: Mixed and conifer woods, parks.

Food: Mainly seeds, berries and green plant material.

Breeding: Mar-Sep, 2 eggs, incubation 16-17 days, young fledge at 28-29 days; 2-3 broods a year. Tree-nester.

2 Rock Dove *Columba livia*

(Pigeons and doves)

In Britain: Jan-Dec.

Identification: 33 cm/330 g. Ancestor of racing and feral pigeons; neck with green and violet iridescence on side, wings pale grey with two dark bars, rump and lower back usually white. Sociable, often in flocks; rarely in trees.

Voice: Muffled cooing *'rucke-di-kuh'* (courtship); *'ruh-ruh-ruh'* (call at nest).

Habitat: Cliff faces with holes, rocky coasts; when feeding, on waste land and cultivated fields.

Food: Mainly seeds and green plant material.

Breeding: Feb-Oct, 2 eggs, incubation 17-18 days, young fledge from about 25 days; 2-3 broods a year. Colonial nester.

3/4 Cuckoo *Cuculus canorus*

(Cuckoos)

In Britain: Apr-Sep.

Identification: 33 cm/110 g. Superficially recalls Sparrowhawk (p. 58) but wings more pointed and longer tailed; underpart barring in male extends to upper breast (Plate 3), in female to chin (Plate 4); reddish-brown ('hepatic') colour phase only in female (Plate 4). Upperparts of young scaly. Solitary; flies with shallow wingbeats, flight silhouette falcon-like.

Voice: Call *'kuckuck'*.

Habitat: In almost all habitats, especially farmland with hedges, woodland edge.

Food: Mainly caterpillars, including hairy caterpillars.

Breeding: Brood parasite; May-Jul, 9-11 eggs (only 1 egg per host nest), incubation by host bird (various passerines) 11-13 days, young fledge at 19-24 days. The young Cuckoo ejects the eggs and young of the host from the nest.

1
2
3|4

1 Kingfisher

Alcedo atthis

(Kingfishers)

In Britain: Jan-Dec.

Identification: 16.5 cm/38 g. Stocky body, large dark bill; upperparts blue and gleaming turquoise, underparts orange-chestnut; female with reddish base to lower mandible. Flight arrow-like, direct; often perches on lookout post over water.

Voice: Call a penetrating *'tiiiit'* or *'tii-tiu'*; when disturbed a repeated *'titititi'*.

Habitat: Clear streams and rivers, especially with steep banks; lakes.

Food: Small fish, larvae of aquatic insects, tadpoles.

Breeding: Apr-Jul, 6-8 eggs, incubation 19-21 days, young fledge at 25 days; 2-3 broods a year. Nests in hole in steep bank.

2 Roller

Coracias garrulus

(Rollers)

In Britain: Rare vagrant.

Identification: 31 cm/140 g. Head, underparts, upper- and underwing coverts turquoise blue, back and shoulders reddish cinnamon-brown, flight feathers and tail blackish, tail with blue terminal band. Sexes similar. Agile display flight with dives and sharp turns; often sits on exposed perch.

Voice: Call a harsh *'rack-rack'*, *'racke-rak'*; in display flight *'rerrerrerr'*; alarm call *'errr'* or *'kraah'*.

Habitat: Open countryside with trees, open deciduous and conifer woods.

Food: Large insects, small reptiles, frogs and mice, berries.

Breeding: May-Jul, 3-5 eggs, incubation 18-19 days, young fledge at 26-28 days. Nests in hole in earth bank or tree hole.

3 Bee-eater

Merops apiaster

(Bee-eaters)

In Britain: May-Sep; vagrant, has bred.

Identification: 28 cm/55 g. Upperparts chestnut-brown, underparts greenish-blue, chin and throat bright yellow, long downcurved bill, pointed tail. Sexes similar. Sociable; flight swallow-like and agile, interspersed with glides on triangular wings with black trailing edge.

Voice: Voice a ringing *'biurr-biurr'* or *'rewpp'* (mostly in flight); alarm call *'dickdickdick'*.

Habitat: Open countryside with isolated trees and bushes.

Food: Large flying insects, especially bees and wasps.

Breeding: May-Jul, 5-7 eggs, incubation 20-22 days, young fledge at 31-33 days. Colonial breeder in earth banks.

1 Hoopoe

Upupa epops

(Hoopoes)

In Britain: Mar-Sep; very scarce visitor, has bred.

Identification: 28 cm/65 g. Fan-like erectile crest with black tips to the feathers, long, slim, downcurved bill; wings and tail broadly barred black-and-white, rest of plumage pale orange-brown. Sexes similar. Flight appears butterfly-like on weak irregular wingbeats; on landing and when excited erects crest; runs on the ground with jerky head movements, often probes in ground.

Voice: A muffled, far-carrying three-syllable *'hubhubhub'*; when agitated a croaking *'khrii'*.

Habitat: Open woodland clearings, parkland, open countryside; in southern Europe common in villages.

Food: Large insects, worms, snails, small lizards and frogs.

Breeding: Apr-Jul, 5-8 eggs, incubation 15-17 days, young fledge at 24-27 days; nestlings squirt watery excrement at intruders as well as producing a foul-smelling secretion from the preen gland. Hole nester.

2 Wryneck

Jynx torquilla

(Woodpeckers)

In Britain: Apr-Oct; now rare.

Identification: 16.5 cm/35 g. Small, slim woodpecker-like bird with bark-coloured plumage; underparts pale brown with fine dark brown barring; feet as in woodpeckers with two toes directed forwards and two back. Sexes similar. Does not climb, seeks food on the ground; flight undulating.

Voice: Both sexes sing a monotonous repeated *'gyegyegye'* crescendo; warning call near nest a noisy *'tetete'*.

Habitat: Open deciduous woodland, orchards, parks, river valleys.

Food: Mainly ants and ant pupae, which it gathers with its long sticky woodpecker-like tongue; also other insects.

Breeding: May-Jul, 7-11 eggs, incubation 12-14 days, young fledge at 20-22 days; 1-2 broods a year. Hole nester. As a late arrival from its African wintering grounds it finds most nest holes already occupied by other species and therefore often ejects the foreign nest along with eggs and young. It brings in no nest material.

1 Black Woodpecker

Dryocopus martius

(Woodpeckers)

In Britain: Not recorded.

Identification: 46 cm/300 g. Long-necked slender crow-sized bird; plumage black, relieved only by bright red crown; bill and eye pale yellow; female with red restricted to hind crown. Young not so intense black.

Voice: Call *'kliuh'*; in spring a rapid repeated *'kvikvikvi'*; in flight *'krukrukru'*; drumming lasts about 2.5 seconds with relatively slow beats.

Habitat: Open mature forest with stands of old timber.

Food: Beetle larvae, ants and ant pupae, which it searches for especially in tree stumps.

Breeding: Apr-Jun, 4-6 eggs, incubation 12-14 days, young fledge at 27-28 days. Hole nester, entrance hole a tall oval.

2 Grey-headed Woodpecker

Picus canus

(Woodpeckers)

In Britain: Not recorded.

Identification: 26 cm/130 g. Head and neck grey, iris red-brown, thin black moustachial stripe, forehead red; female like male but lacking red. Young similar to adults. Seeks food mostly on ground.

Voice: Falling series of 8 to 12 soft piping/whistling notes *'giugiugiu'*, slower at end; quiet *'gliuck'* call; even-tempo drumming, almost two seconds long, 20 beats a second.

Habitat: Open deciduous and mixed woodland, parkland.

Food: Ants and ant pupae, other insects; in winter some seeds and fruits.

Breeding: Apr-Jun, 7-9 eggs, incubation 15-17 days, young fledge at 24-25 days. Hole nester.

3 Green Woodpecker

Picus viridis

(Woodpeckers)

In Britain: Jan-Dec.

Identification: 32 cm/190 g. Extensive red crown extending back on to nape, iris pale yellow, black around eye; male with red, female all black, moustachial stripe. Young speckled. Feeds almost entirely on ground.

Voice: Laughing phrase *'gluckgluckgluck'*; pitch and spacing remaining almost steady; drums very rarely, of short duration.

Habitat: Open deciduous woodland, parkland, orchards.

Food: Almost entirely ants and ant pupae, which it catches with its sticky tongue.

Breeding: Apr-Jun, 5-8 eggs, incubation 15-19 days, young fledge at 23-27 days. Hole nester, entrance hole a broad oval.

1 Great Spotted Woodpecker

(Woodpeckers)   *Dendrocopos major*

In Britain: Jan-Dec.

Identification: 23 cm/80 g. Strongly contrasting plumage, black moustache extends back to nape, underparts pure white, undertail coverts bright red, white shoulder patches, red patch on nape; female lacking red on head; young with red crown.

Voice: Call a hard *'kick'*; in courtship a hoarse *'ririri'*; drumming about half a second long, accelerating with each blow.

Habitat: Woods, parkland, orchards.

Food: Wood-dwelling insects and larvae; in winter also nuts and conifer seeds; it jams nuts and cones into crevices in tree trunks to open them; tree sap.

Breeding: May-Jun, 5-7 eggs, incubation 12 days, young fledge at 18-24 days. Hole nester.

2 Middle Spotted Woodpecker

(Woodpeckers)   *Dendrocopos medius*

In Britain: Not recorded.

Identification: 22 cm/60 g. Crown bright pale red, no black moustache; flanks streaked black, undertail coverts pink, white shoulder patches; female with pinkish-red crown. Young similar to adults.

Voice: Call *'gegegege'*, *'kiuk'*; during pair-formation a hoarse squawking *'quiii'*; drums very rarely, slow.

Habitat: Deciduous woods and parkland with old oaks and hornbeams.

Food: Insects and wood-dwelling larvae, nuts, seeds.

Breeding: Apr-Jun, 5-6 eggs, incubation 12 days, young fledge at 22-23 days. Hole nester.

3 Lesser Spotted Woodpecker

(Woodpeckers)   *Dendrocopos minor*

In Britain: Jan-Dec.

Identification: 14.5 cm/22 g. Smallest European woodpecker; upperparts black with white barring, underparts whitish, streaked black, crown red; crown of female whitish; young with dirty white crown.

Voice: High *'kikikiki'*; drumming prolonged, 1-2 seconds long, with relatively slow, even beats.

Habitat: Deciduous and mixed woods, parkland.

Food: Insects on twigs and leaves, wood-dwelling larvae.

Breeding: Apr-Jun, 4-6 eggs, incubation 11 days, young fledge at 19-21 days. Hole nester.

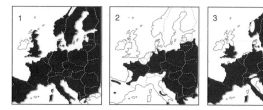

PIGEONS AND WOODPECKERS
Silhouettes of birds perched and in flight

Woodpigeon

Rock Dove

Collared Dove

Turtle Dove

Woodpigeon

Rock Dove

Stock Dove

Collared Dove

Turtle Dove

Great Spotted Woodpecker

Green Woodpecker

Black Woodpecker

Lesser Spotted Woodpecker

Grey-headed Woodpecker

Wryneck

PASSERINES 1
Silhouettes of corvids perched and in flight

Jackdaw

Rook

Carrion Crow

Hooded Crow

Raven

Jay

Nutcracker

Alpine Chough

1 Crested Lark

Galerida cristata

(Larks)

In Britain: Rare vagrant.

Identification: 17 cm/45 g. Stocky, short-tailed, streaking less strongly contrasting than on Skylark; pointed crest, bill relatively long. Sexes similar. Sings mostly from the ground, rarely in circling song flight; not shy.

Voice: Call a melodic *'diedidriye'* and *'diu diu diur dli'*. Song: many whistling notes and mimicry of other birds, divided up by pauses.

Habitat: Fallow land, steppes, semi-deserts, edge of towns, railway embankments.

Food: Seeds, green plant material, insects.

Breeding: Apr-Jun, 3-5 eggs, incubation 13 days, young fledge at 9-10 days; double-brooded. Nests on ground.

2 Skylark

Alauda arvensis

(Larks)

In Britain: Jan-Dec.

Identification: 18 cm/40 g. Upperparts streaked pale and dark brown, underparts whitish. Breast streaked; relatively long tail with white outer tail feathers; short erectile crest. Sexes similar. Hovers in high song flight more or less in the same spot.

Voice: Call *'tirr'* or *'tschrl'*, when migrating *'tsitsi'*. Song in flight, up to 15 minutes without pause, trilling and warbling, with mimicry of other birds.

Habitat: Open, spacious landscapes, in southern Europe also mountains.

Food: Seeds, green plant material, insects, spiders.

Breeding: Apr-Jul, 3-4 eggs, incubation 11-14 days, young leave nest at 9-10 days, fledge at about 20 days; double-brooded. Nests on ground.

3 Woodlark

Lullula arborea

(Larks)

In Britain: Jan-Dec.

Identification: 15 cm/26 g. Short-tailed with weak bill, whitish supercilia, meeting on nape, black-and-white mark on edge of wing. Sexes similar. Sings from tree or in high, undulating, circling song flight, also by night.

Voice: Call *'titroit'*, *'dadidloi'*. Song: melancholy soft fluting, consisting of many varied short phrases in rapid succession.

Habitat: Dry woodland clearings, conifer woods, heaths.

Food: Insects, spiders, seeds, green plant material.

Breeding: Mar-Jul, 3-5 eggs, incubation 12-15 days, young fledge at 12-15 days; 2-3 broods a year. Nests on ground.

1

2

3

1   Shore Lark   *Eremophila alpestris*

(Larks)

In Britain: Nov-Apr; has bred.

Identification: 16.5 cm/36 g. Striking facial pattern black and pale yellow, feather 'horns', relatively long tail with white outer tail feathers. Both sexes in winter with scarcely visible horns, less contrasting. Sings from stone perch or in high circling song flight. In winter in small flocks. Turkish race (*penicillata*) with more extensive black on face, less yellow (Plate).

Voice: Call *'tsip'*; in flight *'tsi-di-diu'*. Song: short hurried warbling phrases.

Habitat: Stony tundra, mountains above the tree-line, rocky plateaus.

Food: Insects, spiders, seeds.

Breeding: May-Jul, 3-4 eggs, incubation 11-12 days, young leave nest at 9-12 days, do not fly until 16-18 days; 1-2 broods a year. Nests on ground.

2   Sand Martin   *Riparia riparia*

(Swallows and martins)

In Britain: Mar-Sep.

Identification: 12 cm/14 g. Small, upperparts brown, underparts white with brown breast band, tail unmarked, weakly forked. Sexes similar. Sociable, roosts in large flocks in reedbeds after the breeding season.

Voice: Call *'tschrrip'* and rapidly repeated *'brbrbr'*; when threatened a sharp *'tsier'*. Song: soft twittering.

Habitat: Open countryside with steep banks and sand pits, usually near water; sandy coastal cliffs.

Food: Small flying insects.

Breeding: May-Aug, 4-5 eggs, incubation 12-16 days, young fledge at 20-22 days; double-brooded. Colonial breeder; digs own burrow in sandy earth bank.

3   Crag Martin   *Ptyonoprogne rupestris*

(Swallows and martins)

In Britain: Rare vagrant.

Identification: 15 cm/23 g. Larger than Sand Martin, upperparts brown, underparts sandy, lacking brown breast band, chin finely streaked, tail with white spots, unforked. Sexes similar. Not as sociable as Sand Martin.

Voice: Call *'tit-tit'*, *'pritit'* or *'tsirrr'*. Song: hurried twittering.

Habitat: Mountain regions with rock faces and gorges, coastal cliffs.

Food: Small flying insects.

Breeding: May-Jul, 4-5 eggs, incubation 14 days, young fledge at 25 days; double-brooded. Nests in small loose colonies under rocky overhangs.

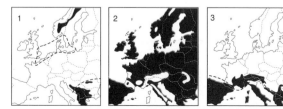

House Martin
Delichon urbica

(Swallows and martins)

In Britain: Apr-Oct.

Identification: 13 cm/20 g. Appears same size as Swallow, tail forked, but lacking tail streamers, upperparts glossy blue-black, white rump visible from a long way off; chin, throat and underparts pure white, feet softly white-feathered. Sexes similar. Young with upperparts brown-black. Sociable; fluttering flight, not as elegant as that of Swallow.

Voice: Call *'trr trr'*, *'dschrb'* or *'briud'*; alarm call a high, piercing *'tsier tsier'*.

Song: short chattering and twittering, lacking purring motif at end; less noticeable and less varied than Swallow.

Habitat: Villages, farmland, rock faces.

Food: Small flying insects.

Breeding: May-Sep, 4-5 eggs, incubation 12-15 days, young fledge at 22-32 days; 2-3 broods a year. Colonial breeder on outside of buildings under eaves, nest a quarter of a ball, neatly mortared, with small entrance hole; originally a cliff nester.

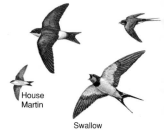

House Martin

Swallow

Swallow
Hirundo rustica

(Swallows and martins)

In Britain: Apr-Oct.

Identification: 19 cm/20 g. Only swallow in our region with long tail streamers; wings narrow and pointed; forehead, chin and throat chestnut, upperparts and breast glossy blue-black, breast, belly and undertail coverts white, tail black with white spots. Sexes similar, but tail streamers of female shorter. Young paler and without streamers. Sociable; agile graceful flight, with deep wingbeats, catches insects on the wing, also takes them from the water surface, and even drinks in dipping flight.

Voice: Call *'vitt vitt'* or *'dsched-dsched'*, alarm call a sharp *'tsivitt tsivitt'*.

Song: hurried phrases, twittering and chattering, with purring motif at end.

Habitat: Villages, isolated buildings, farmland, water-bodies.

Food: Small flying insects.

Breeding: May-Sep, 4-6 eggs, incubation 13-18 days, young fledge at 18-22 days; 2-3 broods a year. Nests in loose colonies in stables and barns; gathers pellets of mud at puddles for nest-building. Nest open above, constructed with mud and grass stems, which often hang down untidily.

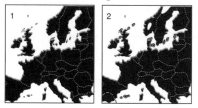

1 Water Pipit

Anthus spinoletta

(Pipits and wagtails)

In Britain: Oct-Apr.

Identification: 16.5 cm/22 g. Upperparts pale grey, whitish supercilia, underparts whitish, unstreaked, breast flushed pink; in winter breast streaked dark. Sexes similar. Wary; song flight.

Voice: Call *'hisst'*, *'psiet'*, alarm a repeated *'tsitt'*. Song: long, accelerating, repeated series of *'tsvi tsvi tsvi'* notes, high and thin.

Habitat: Mountain pastures, high alpine meadows; in winter by lowland water-bodies. *Food:* Mainly insects. *Breeding:* Apr-Jul, 4-5 eggs, incubation 14-16 days, young fledge at 15 days; 1-2 broods a year. Nests on ground.

Similar species: **Rock Pipit** *Anthus petrosus.* Darker, smoky-brown plumage, heavily streaked above and below; dark legs (Plate 4). Lives around coasts of northwest Europe.

2 Tree Pipit

Anthus trivialis

(Pipits and wagtails)

In Britain: Apr-Sep.

Identification: 15 cm/22 g. Upperparts pale brown, weakly streaked, underparts pale cream, breast yellowish-brown with dark streaking. Sings from tree tops and in song flight, usually returning to same perch.

Voice: Call a high hoarse *'psieh'*, alarm *'tsipp-tsipp'*. Song: loud warbling and twittering with trills and whistling figures such as *'tsiatsia-tsia-tsia'*, *'uiui-ui-ui'*.

Habitat: Open countryside with trees, woodland edge and clearings. *Food:* Mainly insects. *Breeding:* May-Jul, 4-6 eggs, incubation 12-13 days, young fledge at 12-14 days; 1-2 broods. Nests on ground.

3 Meadow Pipit

Anthus pratensis

(Pipits and wagtails)

In Britain: Jan-Dec.

Identification: 14.5 cm/18 g. Plumage markings like Tree Pipit, but altogether greyer, hind claw very long. Sexes similar. Usually climbs from the ground in song flight, not returning to the takeoff point. In winter in flocks.

Voice: Call a high *'ist-ist'*. Song: long monotonous phrases of several figures, high and thin, hoarse tinkling, introduced by accelerating *'dip dip'* notes.

Habitat: Damp meadows, moorland, waste ground, dunes. *Food:* Mainly insects. *Breeding:* Apr-Jul, 4-6 eggs, incubation 13 days, young fledge at 12-14 days; double-brooded. Nests on ground.

1

2

3 | 4

1   Tawny Pipit   *Anthus campestris*

(Pipits and wagtails)

In Britain: Scarce visitor.

Identification: 17 cm/23 g. Longer-tailed than Tree Pipit (p. 172); upperparts sandy-coloured, underparts whitish, unstreaked; conspicuous creamy-white stripe over eye. Ground dweller, runs wagtail-like and occasionally wags tail. Sings from prominence on ground or in undulating climbing song flight.

Voice: A variety of calls such as *'tsiehp'*, *'tschlipp'* or *'tsieh'*. Song: continually repeated *'tsirlui'*, *'treih'* or similar.

Habitat: Dry fallow land, steppes, open heaths, sandy banks.

Food: Mainly insects.

Breeding: May-Jul, 4-5 eggs, incubation 12-14 days, young fledge at 15 days; 1-2 broods a year. Nests on ground.

2   Yellow Wagtail   *Motacilla flava*

(Pipits and wagtails)

In Britain: Apr-Sep.

Identification: 16.5 cm/18 g. Shorter-tailed than Pied Wagtail (p. 176), throat and head bright yellow (head blue-grey in Continental race, Plate), upperparts olive-green, underparts sulphur yellow. Female and winter plumage paler. Ground dweller, wags tail, sings occasionally in undulating song flight.

Voice: Call *'psewip'* or *'psiehp'*. Song: repeated *'tsier-tsier'*.

Habitat: Cattle pasture, farmland, marshes, bogs, heaths.

Food: Small insects.

Breeding: Apr-Jul, 5-6 eggs, incubation 13 days, young fledge at 11-13 days; 1-2 broods a year. Nests on ground.

3   Grey Wagtail   *Motacilla cinerea*

(Pipits and wagtails)

In Britain: Jan-Dec.

Identification: 18 cm/18 g. Distinctly longer-tailed than Yellow Wagtail, head and upperparts grey, chin and throat black, underparts pale yellow. In female and winter plumage chin and throat whitish. Wags tail, flight undulating, often low over water. Sings perched or in flight.

Voice: Call more piercing than Pied Wagtail *'tsickick'*, alarm call a high *'tsewih'*. Song: various twittering phrases, with whistling and rolled notes.

Habitat: Streams and rivers in mountains and lowlands.

Food: Insects.

Breeding: Apr-Jul, 4-6 eggs, incubation 12-14 days, young fledge at 12-13 days; double-brooded. Nests in open hole.

1   Pied Wagtail   *Motacilla alba*

(Pipits and wagtails)

In Britain: Jan-Dec.

Identification: 18 cm/22 g. Long-tailed, head and neck black-and-white, upperparts black in British 'Pied Wagtail', grey in Continental race 'White Wagtail' (Plate), underparts white; female a little paler. In winter chin and throat white, blackish breast band. Young pale, without black. Runs with jerky head movements, constantly wagging tail, flight undulating.

Voice: Call *'tsitt'*, *'tsivlitt'* or *'tsipp-tsipp-tsilipp'*. Song: twittering and chattering with elements of call.

Habitat: Open countryside, villages, gardens, mostly near water.

Food: Insects.

Breeding: Apr-Jul, 5-6 eggs, incubation 12-14 days, young fledge at 14-15 days; double-brooded. Nests in open hole.

2   Waxwing   *Bombycilla garrulus*

(Waxwings)

In Britain: Nov-Apr; irregular visitor.

Identification: 18 cm/60 g. Red-brown silky plumage, crested, chin and throat black, wing-coverts decorated with sealing-wax-red tips, tail with yellow terminal band. Female paler. Young with streaked underparts. Sociable, tame, irregular invasion species to central and western Europe in winter.

Voice: Call high *'sirr'*. Song: repeated rattling and wheezing notes.

Habitat: Conifer (especially larch) and birch forest; in winter gardens and parks with berried bushes.

Food: Insects, berries, fruit.

Breeding: Jun-Jul, 4-6 eggs, incubation 12-15 days, young fledge at 14-16 days. Nests in trees in loose colonies.

3   Lesser Grey Shrike   *Lanius minor*

(Shrikes)

In Britain: Vagrant.

Identification: 20 cm/50 g. Similar to Great Grey Shrike (p. 178) but smaller. Upperparts pale grey; broad mask extending over forehead; underparts white with pink flush. Sexes similar.

Voice: When flushed a repeated *'kerrib-kerrib'* or *'tschilip tschilip'*. Song: soft chattering with mimicry of other species.

Habitat: Orchards, avenues of fruit trees, open countryside, vineyards.

Food: Mainly large insects (beetles, grasshoppers, crickets).

Breeding: May-Jul, 4-6 eggs, incubation 15 days, young fledge at 16 days.

176

1

2

3

Great Grey Shrike

Lanius excubitor

(Shrikes)

In Britain: Oct-Apr.

Identification: 24 cm/65 g. Largest shrike, thrush-sized; head and back pale grey, black mask, underparts white, white patch in wing. Sexes similar.

Voice: When disturbed a sharp two or three syllable *'ved'*, also Magpie-like chacking. Song: harsh notes and whistles, often with mimicry of other birds.

Habitat: Open countryside with groups of trees, bogs, heaths; orchards, hedges.

Food: Large insects, mice, small birds.

Breeding: Apr-Jun, 5-6 eggs, incubation 15 days, young fledge at 15-20 days. Tree-nester.

Red-backed Shrike

Lanius collurio

(Shrikes)

In Britain: May-Oct; now only scarce migrant.

Identification: 17 cm/30 g. Male head ash-grey with thick black mask, back chestnut, underparts peachy-white; female without mask, upperparts brownish, underparts barred. Skewers prey on thorns and barbs.

Voice: Call an agitated *'dschi'* or *'trrt-trrt'*, when disturbed at nest a hard *'tek'* or *'dschrii'*. Song: hurried warbling and mumbling with much mimicry; seldom heard.

Habitat: Open countryside with hedges and thorn thickets; woodland edge, bogs and heaths.

Food: Large insects, also small frogs and lizards, young birds, small mammals.

Breeding: May-Jul, 4-6 eggs, incubation 14-16 days, young fledge at 15 days. Nests in thorn thickets.

Woodchat Shrike

Lanius senator

(Shrikes)

In Britain: Apr-Oct; scarce visitor, does not breed.

Identification: 18 cm/35 g. Size of Red-backed Shrike, but looks stockier and bigger-headed; male with crown and nape rusty-red, forehead black, back and wings black, underparts white. Female similar to male but paler.

Voice: When disturbed a rattling *'dsched-dsched'* or *'dsche-dsche'*, aggressive sonorous *'griug'*. Song: continuous melodious chattering interspersed with harsh notes and mimicry.

Habitat: Open countryside with trees, orchards.

Food: Large insects.

Breeding: May-Jul, 4-6 eggs, incubation 15 days, young fledge at 14-16 days. Tree-nester.

1

2|3

1 Dunnock

Prunella modularis

(Accentors)

In Britain: Jan.-Dec.

Identification: 14.5 cm/20 g. Size of House Sparrow (p. 238), but much slimmer and with thin bill; plumage grey-brown, head and breast lead-grey. Sexes similar. Hops along ground in hunched posture; flitting flight.

Voice: Call a high *'tsieh'*; in flight *'dididi'*. Song: rolling thin warbling, recalling Serin (p. 234) or Wren (p. 220), but without trilling phrase; starts singing early in year (March) from exposed perch.

Habitat: Mixed and conifer woods and plantations, parkland, gardens and cemeteries.

Food: Soft-bodied insects and spiders; in autumn and winter mainly small seeds, comes to bird tables.

Breeding: Apr-Jul, 4-5 eggs, incubation 13 days, young fledge at 11-14 days; double-brooded. Nest of moss in dense cover, often conifers.

2 Alpine Accentor

Prunella collaris

(Accentors)

In Britain: Rare vagrant.

Identification: 18 cm/40 g. Distinctly larger and stockier than Dunnock, lark-like jizz; head grey, chin and throat whitish with blackish scaling, back grey-brown, flanks with red-brown streaking. Sexes similar. Young without scaling on throat. Hops rapidly and nimbly, when excited bobs and jerks tail vigorously.

Voice: Call a high *'driurr'*, often repeated; also *'tsak-tsak'*, *'trui'* and in flight a chirping *'schirr'*. Song: Skylark-like, slower than Dunnock, consisting of hard deep trills and chattering notes.

Habitat: Alpine zone of high mountains, mostly at altitude of 1500 to 2300 m; sparsely vegetated plateaus with rocks and scree; in winter in valleys.

Food: Insects, in autumn and winter also small seeds and berries.

Breeding: May-Jun, 3-5 eggs, incubation 13-15 days, young fledge at 16 days. Nests on ground.

1 Cetti's Warbler

Cettia cetti

(Warblers)

In Britain: Jan-Dec.
Identification: 13.5 cm/male 15-16 g, female 12 g. Dark rufous-brown above, pale grey below; short wings, long rounded tail, often cocked. Male much heavier than female (very unusual in passerines).
Voice: Very loud, explosive *'chi chewi chewi chewi'*, delivered at intervals from dense cover. *Habitat:* Dense vegetation, usually near water.
Food: Insects, other invertebrates. *Breeding:* Jun-Jul, 4-5 eggs, incubation 16-17 days, young fledge at 14-16 days.

2 Grasshopper Warbler

Locustella naevia

(Warblers)

In Britain: Apr-Aug.
Identification: 13 cm/14 g. Upperparts olive-brown, streaked darker, underparts dirty grey. Keeps in low cover, mostly in tall grass, scurrying or walking mouse-like.
Voice: Call a sharp *'tze tze'* or *'tschick'*. Song: extended buzzing *'sirrr'*, very similar to grasshopper reeling. *Habitat:* Marshy meadows with bushes, fallow land with willows and alders, bogs. *Food:* Insects and spiders.
Breeding: May-Jul, 4-6 eggs, incubation 13 days, young fledge at 11 days; 1-2 broods a year. Nests on ground.

3 Savi's Warbler

Locustella luscinioides

(Warblers)

In Britain: Apr-Aug; rare.
Identification: 14 cm/16 g. Larger than Grasshopper Warbler, reddish-brown (like Nightingale, p. 204), with no streaking above or below. Sexes similar.
Voice: Call a sharp *'tsick'*, when disturbed at nest *'pit pit'*. Song: similar to Grasshopper Warbler, but less sustained and not purely consonantal, but distinctly vowel-coloured *'irrrrr'*. *Habitat:* Silted fringes of water-bodies with reed, sedge and rush. Much more strictly associated with water than Grasshopper Warbler. *Food:* Insects and spiders.
Breeding: May-Jul, 4-6 eggs, incubation 12 days, young fledge at 12-14 days; double-brooded. Nests low down in reeds.
Similar species: **River Warbler** *Locustella fluviatilis* (Plate 4). Small than Savi's, throat and breast with indistinct streaking.. Song a continuous rhythmical sharpening sound. Inhabits riverine forest in Eastern Europe.

1 Reed Warbler
Acrocephalus scirpaceus
(Warblers)

In Britain: Apr-Oct.
Identification: 13 cm/12 g. Very difficult to tell apart from same-sized Marsh Warbler; plumage however reddish-brown, not olive. Sexes similar.
Voice: When disturbed a hard *'ved'*. Song: similar to Great Reed Warbler but much more continuous, softer and more hurried, consisting of seamless series of motifs, each repeated two or three times.
Habitat: Reed fringe of water-bodies, willows on river banks.
Food: Insects, spiders.
Breeding: May-Aug, 3-5 eggs, incubation 10-13 days, young fledge at 10-12 days. Nest suspended between reed-stems.

2 Marsh Warbler
Acrocephalus palustris
(Warblers)

In Britain: May-Sep; rare breeder.
Identification: 13 cm/12 g. Size and shape of Reed Warbler, but plumage olive-brown, not reddish-brown, legs usually paler (flesh-coloured). Sexes similar.
Voice: When alarmed a hard *'tak'* or *'ved'*. Song: very varied and melodious, not organised into phrases, consisting of grating, scolding and chirping with much mimicry of other birds, such as Blue Tit, Swallow and Bluethroat.
Habitat: Willow scrub and nettle patches on river banks and ditches, cereal fields.
Food: Insects, spiders.
Breeding: May-Jul, 4-5 eggs, incubation 13 days, young fledge at 10-12 days. Nest suspended in thick vegetation.

3 Great Reed Warbler
Acrocephalus arundinaceus
(Warblers)

In Britain: May-Sep; rare visitor, does not breed.
Identification: 19 cm/30 g. Largest European reed warbler; deep red-brown, throat and underparts paler. Sexes similar.
Voice: When alarmed a deep *'karr'*. Song: far-carrying grating, consisting of distinctly separated short phrases such as *'karre karre karre kiet kiet dorre dorre'*.
Habitat: Extensive reed-beds by lakes and ponds.
Food: Insects, spiders, tiny frogs.
Breeding: May-Jul, 4-6 eggs, incubation 13-15 days, young fledge at 12-14 days; 1-2 broods a year. Nest suspended between reed-stems.

3

1 Sedge Warbler
Acrocephalus schoenobaenus
(Warblers)

In Britain: Apr-Sep.
Identification: 13 cm/12 g. Conspicuously dark-streaked upperparts, pale supercilia, rump pale reddish-brown. Sexes similar.
Voice: When alarmed a hard *'tsrrr'*, or *'karr'*. Song: similar to Reed Warbler (p. 184) but not so uniform, more varied with much mimicry and a typical *'void-void-void'* phrase; often in short song flight.
Habitat: Reed-beds and thick bankside vegetation.
Food: Insects, spiders.
Breeding: May-Jul, 5-6 eggs, incubation 13 days, young fledge at 12-14 days; double-brooded. Nests on or up to 50 cm above ground, in reeds.

2 Fan-tailed Warbler
Cisticola juncidis
(Warblers)

In Britain: Rare vagrant.
Identification: 10 cm/9 g. Very small; upperparts yellowish-brown with strong streaking, tail short and graduated. Sexes similar.
Voice: When disturbed a tuneless short *'pt-pt-pt'*; also a soft *'tyu'*. Song: penetrating, continuously repeated *'tsip-tsip-tsip'*, mostly given in song flight.
Habitat: Damp coastal plains, grassland, marshes.
Food: Insects and spiders.
Breeding: Apr-Aug, 4-6 eggs, incubation 12-13 days, young fledge at 14-15 days; double-brooded. Suspended nest in low vegetation.

3 Icterine Warbler
Hippolais icterina
(Warblers)

In Britain: May-Sep; scarce migrant.
Identification: 13.5 cm/13 g. Like a large yellow-green leaf-warbler, but more powerful, with long broad orange-coloured bill. Sexes similar.
Voice: When excited *'dederoid'*, alarm call a smacking *'tze tze tze'*. Song: continuous, unstructured, with repeated melodic motifs and mimicry.
Habitat: Open deciduous woodland, copses, gardens, parkland.
Food: Insects and spiders; in autumn also berries.
Breeding: May-Jul, 4-6 eggs, incubation 12-14 days, young fledge at 13 days. Nests in bushes and young trees.
Similar species: **Melodious Warbler** *Hippolais polyglotta*. Very similar to Icterine Warbler, but underparts vary from rich yellow to cream-coloured. Breeds in Iberia, France, Italy and southern Switzerland. Scarce autumn migrant to south coast of Britain.

1 Whitethroat

Sylvia communis

(Warblers)

In Britain: Apr-Sep.

Identification: 14 cm/15 g. Male with crown and cheeks pale grey, throat pure white, upperparts grey-brown, wings rusty-brown, underparts with peachy suffusion; female with brownish head, underparts lacking peachy suffusion.

Voice: Call *'tek'*, *'void void'* and *'dscharp'*. Song: short, harsh chattering with scratching or grinding tone-colour; short song flight.

Habitat: Thorn scrub and thorny hedges bordering fields.

Food: Insects, spiders, berries.

Breeding: May-Jul, 4-6 eggs, incubation 12 days, young fledge at 11-12 days; double-brooded. Nests low in thorn scrub.

Similar species: **Subalpine Warbler** *Sylvia cantillans*. Throat and breast reddish brown, striking white moustachial stripe, red eye-ring, white outer tail feathers; often cocks tail. Breeds in Mediterranean.

2 Lesser Whitethroat

Sylvia curruca

(Warblers)

In Britain: Apr-Oct.

Identification: 13.5 cm/12 g. Like small Whitethroat, very similar in colour, but ear-coverts dark grey, underparts not peachy, but with brownish wash, wings lacking rufous. Sexes similar. Dark legs.

Voice: Call a smacking *'tek'*, alarm call in flight a short *'ved'*. Song: a loud monotonous wooden rattling phrase following a soft hoarse warble.

Habitat: Gardens, parks, copses, woodland edge.

Food: Insects; in autumn also berries.

Breeding: May-Jul, 4-6 eggs, incubation 12 days, young fledge at 12 days. Nests in low scrub.

3 Garden Warbler

Sylvia borin

(Warblers)

In Britain: Apr-Oct.

Identification: 14 cm/20 g. A little bigger and stockier than Blackcap (p. 190); uniform olive-brown with paler underparts. Sexes similar.

Voice: Alarm call *'vet vet'* or *'tzeck tzeck'*. Song: continuous phrases in bubbling chattering delivery with deep organ-like notes; Blackbird-like tone.

Habitat: Open deciduous and mixed woodland, gardens, parks.

Food: Insects, spiders and berries.

Breeding: May-Jul, 4-5 eggs, incubation 11-13 days, young fledge at 10-12 days. Nests low in bramble or nettle patch.

1

2

3

Blackcap

(Warblers)

Sylvia atricapilla

In Britain: Jan-Dec.
Identification: 14 cm/18 g. Male upperparts grey-brown, underparts ash-grey, skullcap black; female with brownish underparts, red-brown cap.
Voice: Call when disturbed a hard *'tak'* or *'tzek'*. Song: begins with hurried warbling notes and ends in loud musical flute-like whistling phrase.
Habitat: Conifer plantations, gardens, parks, copses, woodland edge.
Food: Insects and spiders; in autumn many berries, especially elderberries.
Breeding: May-Jul, 4-6 eggs, incubation 11-12 days, young fledge at 10-13 days; 1-2 broods. Nests in low scrub.
Similar species: **Sardinian Warbler** *Sylvia melanocephala*. A little smaller than Blackcap, top and sides of head jet-black, red eye-ring. Resident in Mediterranean.

Barred Warbler

(Warblers)

Sylvia nisoria

In Britain: Aug-Oct; scarce migrant.
Identification: 15 cm/24 g. Larger than Blackcap; upperparts brown-grey, underparts whitish with grey barring (like Sparrowhawk), eye piercing yellow. Female like male, but browner and paler. Young without barring.
Voice: Call when disturbed *'tr tr'* or *'dididi'*. Song: like Garden Warbler, but phrases shorter with harsh *'errr'* noises and deep fluty notes.
Habitat: Woodland edge with thorn bushes, juniper heaths.
Food: Insects, spiders, berries.
Breeding: May-Jul, 4-6 eggs, incubation 12-14 days, young fledge at 10-12 days. Nests in thorn thickets.

Dartford Warbler

(Warblers)

Sylvia undata

In Britain: Jan-Dec.
Identification: 12.5 cm/9 g. Very small dark warbler with long tail, often cocked; throat with fine white streaking; red eye-ring. Female like male, but paler.
Voice: Call a nasal extended *'djerr'* or chattering *'trtrtrtr'*. Song: short, hurried phrases of rattling and piping elements, Whitethroat-like.
Habitat: Maquis and garrigue (dry evergreen scrub of the Mediterranean), lowland heaths.
Food: Insects, spiders, berries.
Breeding: Apr-Jul, 3-6 eggs, incubation 12-13 days, young fledge at 12 days. Nests low in heather or gorse.

1   Willow Warbler

Phylloscopus trochilus

(Warblers)

In Britain: Apr-Sep.

Identification: 11 cm/9 g. Size and jizz of Chiffchaff, but plumage tones yellower, with distinct pale stripe over eye and dark eyestripe; legs usually pale flesh colour. Sexes similar.

Voice: Call a disyllabic *'hu-id'*. Song: soft falling phrase of pure notes of melancholy character.

Habitat: Light woodland, copses, thin birch stands in bogs, plantations, gardens.

Food: Insects and spiders.

Breeding: May-Jun, 4-7 eggs, incubation 13 days, young fledge at 13 days. Dome-shaped nest on ground.

2   Chiffchaff

Phylloscopus collybita

(Warblers)

In Britain: Jan-Dec.

Identification: 11 cm/8 g. Very similar to the closely-related Willow Warbler, but less yellow, more olive-brown, legs always dark. Sexes similar.

Voice: Call monosyllabic soft *'heud'*. Song: long stammering phrases of two interchangeable elements *'tsilp-tsalp-tselp-tsilp-tsalp'*.

Habitat: Open deciduous and mixed woodland, copses, gardens, parks.

Food: Insects and spiders.

Breeding: Apr-Jun, 5-6 eggs, incubation 14 days, young fledge at 14-16 days; 1-2 broods a year. Dome-shaped nest close to ground.

3   Wood Warbler

Phylloscopus sibilatrix

(Warblers)

In Britain: Apr-Sep.

Identification: 13 cm/10 g. Largest European leaf-warbler; upperparts yellowish-green, conspicuous sulphur yellow stripe over eye, throat and breast sulphur yellow, belly white. Sexes similar.

Voice: When disturbed a soft *'diuh'*. Song: buzzing phrase, which begins with an accelerating *'sip sip sip'* and ends in a monotonous shivering trill; often given in short level song flight; alternative song phrase of plaintive fluty notes *'diu-diu-diu'*.

Habitat: Favours mature beech forest, sessile oak woods.

Food: Insects and spiders.

Breeding: May-Jun, 5-7 eggs, incubation 13 days, young fledge at 12-13 days. Dome-shaped nest on ground.

Bonelli's Warbler *Phylloscopus bonelli*

(Warblers)

In Britain: Vagrant.

Identification: 11.5 cm/8 g. Size and colour of Chiffchaff (p. 192), but greyer, throat and underparts silky white. Sexes similar.

Voice: Call a disyllabic *'ho-ihd'*. Song: short buzzing phrase of 7 to 13 elements on same pitch, recalling the shivering trill of Wood Warbler (p. 192), but somewhat slower and without an introduction.

Habitat: Conifer and mixed woods on sunny hillsides up to the tree-line.

Food: Insects and spiders.

Breeding: May-Jun, 5-6 eggs, incubation 13 days, young fledge at 12 days. Nests on ground.

Goldcrest *Regulus regulus*

(Warblers)

In Britain: Jan-Dec.

Identification: 9 cm/5 g. Tiny, along with Firecrest the smallest European bird; orange-red (male) or yellow (female) central crown, bordered at sides with black stripes.

Voice: Call high and thin *'sih-sih-sih'*. Song: short phrases of very high-pitched notes, which clearly alternate in pitch, finishing with a flourish.

Habitat: Conifer woods, especially spruce, mixed woods, parkland.

Food: Insects, spiders.

Breeding: Apr-Jun, 8-10 eggs, incubation 16 days, young fledge at 19 days; double-brooded. Suspended nest in conifer.

Firecrest *Regulus ignicapillus*

(Warblers)

In Britain: Jan-Dec; scarce.

Identification: 9 cm/5 g. Very similar to the commoner Goldcrest, but more brightly coloured; black stripe through and white stripe over eye, crown in male orange-red, in female yellow, bordered black on both sides and on forehead; sides of neck golden-bronze.

Voice: Call a more piercing *'sisisi'* than Goldcrest. Song: crescendo of short phrases on a level pitch, with an emphatic final trill.

Habitat: Conifer, mixed and deciduous woods.

Food: Insects, spiders.

Breeding: May-Jul, 7-12 eggs, incubation 14-17 days, young fledge at 20-24 days; double-brooded. Suspended nest in conifer.

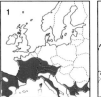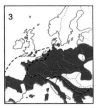

Spotted Flycatcher
Muscicapa striata

(Flycatchers)

In Britain: May-Oct.

Identification: 14 cm/16 g. Inconspicuous grey-brown coloured flycatcher; forehead and breast streaked. Sexes similar. Very slender, sits upright, hunts insects from a lookout perch, flicking its wings after alighting.

Voice: Call a restrained *'tsieh'* or *'pst'*. Song: easily overlooked clipped high notes *'tsitsi sir tsriu tzr'*.

Habitat: Open deciduous woods, parkland, gardens, cemeteries.

Food: Almost entirely flying insects.

Breeding: May-Jul, 4-6 eggs, incubation 13 days, young fledge at 12-15 days; 1-2 broods a year. Nests in open hole.

Collared Flycatcher
Ficedula albicollis

(Flycatchers)

In Britain: Rare vagrant.

Identification: 13 cm/13 g. Male like Pied Flycatcher, but with white neck collar, white rump and broader white patch in wing; female grey-brown, forehead and wing patch white.

Voice: When disturbed a fine *'sieb'* or *'fiit'*; also a short *'tk'*. Song: thin and high in slow tempo, usually begins with *'fiit'* and ends with deeper piping notes.

Habitat: As Pied Flycatcher.

Food: Insects, which it hunts in the tree canopy.

Breeding: May-Jul, 4-7 eggs, incubation 13 days, young fledge at 16 days. Hole-nester.

Pied Flycatcher
Ficedula hypoleuca

(Flycatchers)

In Britain: Apr-Oct.

Identification: 13 cm/13 g. Somewhat smaller and stockier than Spotted Flycatcher; male with upperparts black, underparts, forehead and wing patch white; males from central and eastern Europe with browner upperparts. Female brown-grey with paler underparts.

Voice: Call *'bitt'* or warning *'tzeck'*. Song: short phrases of disyllabic repeated notes *'vutivutivuti'*.

Habitat: Deciduous and mixed woods, gardens, parks.

Food: Insects, caught in flight or gathered from the foliage of trees.

Breeding: May-Jun, 6-8 eggs, incubation 13 days, young fledge at 16 days. Hole-nester.

Red-breasted Flycatcher
Ficedula parva

(Flycatchers)

In Britain: Sep-Oct; scarce migrant.

Identification: 11.5 cm/10 g. Male similar to Robin (p. 202) in colour, but smaller and more dainty; typical short-legged flycatcher, often flicks its tail revealing white patches at base. Male throat and breast red; female and young males lacking red.

Voice: Call a Wren-like *'tsirrr'*; when agitated a high *'tsit'*; when disturbed *'diuli'*. Song: descending phrase of pure notes, recalling song of Willow Warbler (p. 192).

Habitat: Deciduous woods, especially mature beech forest.

Food: Flying insects, hunted high in the canopy.

Breeding: May-Jul, 5-7 eggs, incubation 13 days, young fledge at 13-14 days. Nests in open hole.

Whinchat
Saxicola rubetra

(Thrushes and chats)

In Britain: Apr-Sep.

Identification: 13 cm/18 g. Stocky bird with short tail; male (Plate 2) with upperparts striped brown, white shoulder patches, broad white supercilia and white moustache, underparts apricot; female (Plate 3) duller. Flicks wings and tail.

Voice: When disturbed a hard *'tk tk'* alternating with a soft *'diu'*. Song: short disjointed song of hoarse scratching and piping notes.

Habitat: Meadows, moorland, open countryside with gorse and scrub.

Food: Flying and ground-dwelling insects.

Breeding: May-Jul, 5-6 eggs, incubation 12-14 days, young fledge from 13 days. Nests on ground.

Stonechat
Saxicola torquata

(Thrushes and chats)

In Britain: Jan-Dec.

Identification: 13 cm/15 g. Similar to Whinchat in jizz and behaviour; male with black head, white patches on sides of neck, black-brown back, white in wing, rusty-orange underparts; female paler, browner.

Voice: When excited *'krr'*; when disturbed *'fid'* or a combined *'fid-krr-krr'* or *'fid-tak-tak'*. Song: short hoarse song of thin quivering whistles and scratchy notes.

Habitat: Juniper heaths, moorland, sandpits, embankments.

Food: Insects.

Breeding: Apr-Jul, 5-6 eggs, incubation 14 days, young fledge at 12-16 days; double-brooded. Nests on ground.

1

2|3

4

Blue Rock Thrush

Monticola solitarius

(Thrushes and chats)

In Britain: Rare vagrant.

Identification: 20 cm/65 g. Male dark blue-grey, bill and legs dark grey; female dark grey-brown, with fine scaling on upper- and underparts.

Voice: When disturbed a hard *'tak-tak'*; pure whistling *'yiu'*. Song: short loud whistling phrases comprising sequence of falling notes; also given in flight.

Habitat: Rocky mountain slopes and sea coasts, quarries, also in settlements.

Food: Insects, spiders, worms, berries.

Breeding: Apr-Jun, 3-5 eggs, incubation 13 days, young fledge at 18 days; 1-2 broods a year. Nests in hole in rocks.

Rock Thrush

Monticola saxatilis

(Thrushes and chats)

In Britain: Rare vagrant.

Identification: 19 cm/55 g. Smaller than Blue Rock Thrush, shorter-billed and shorter-tailed. Male with head and neck grey-blue, underparts rusty-red, rump white, tail rufous; in winter plumage head and underparts with whitish fringes to feathers; female brown with strong scaling.

Voice: When disturbed a Redstart-like *'tack tack'* and *'yiu'*. Song: pleasant whistling phrases, often in song flight.

Habitat: Dry, sunny rocky slopes, quarries, ruins.

Food: Insects, spiders, worms, berries.

Breeding: May-Jun, 4-5 eggs, incubation 13-15 days, young fledge at 13-16 days. Nests in hole in rocks

Wheatear

Oenanthe oenanthe

(Thrushes and chats)

In Britain: Mar-Oct.

Identification: 15 cm/25 g. Male with crown and back pale grey, pale stripe over eye, sides of head black; underparts, throat and breast creamy-coloured; rump and base of tail white; female and young brownish-cream.

Voice: When excited a hard *'tk tk tk'* and single *'fid'* note. Song: short chattering and murmuring phrases, mixed with whistles.

Habitat: Open, stony countryside, waste ground, dunes, scree, vineyards.

Food: Insects and spiders. *Breeding:* Apr-Jul, 5-6 eggs, incubation 14 days, young fledge at 15 days. Nests in hole in ground or wall.

Similar species: **Black-eared Wheatear** *Oenanthe hispanica*. Like Wheatear but upper- and underparts buff-coloured or creamy-white. One form with black throat. Inhabits stony, dry countryside in southern Europe.

1   Black Redstart

Phoenicurus ochruros

(Thrushes and chats)

In Britain: Jan-Dec; scarce.

Identification: 14 cm/16 g. Sooty black, crown and back dark ash-grey, whitish patch in wings, tail and rump rusty-red; female dark grey-brown, tail and rump rusty-red.

Voice: Call when excited *'hid teck teck'*. Song: begins with several high whistling notes, followed by a squeezed scratching hiss and some further whistles.

Habitat: Rocky slopes and cliffs in mountains, buildings in villages and towns.

Food: Insects and spiders.

Breeding: Apr-Jul, 4-6 eggs, incubation 13 days, young fledge at about 15 days; double-brooded. Nests in open hole.

2   Redstart

Phoenicurus phoenicurus

(Thrushes and chats)

In Britain: Apr-Oct.

Identification: 14 cm/15 g. Male with forehead gleaming white, throat and sides of head black, upperparts slate-grey, underparts, rump and tail rusty-red; female brownish with paler underparts.

Voice: Call when agitated *'huid-teck-teck'*. Song: starts with a drawn-out whistling note, followed by a short series of short deeper ringing notes *'yiu tri tri ...'*; tone-colour like song of Pied Flycatcher (p. 196).

Habitat: Open deciduous and mixed woodland, gardens, parks.

Food: Insects and spiders.

Breeding: May-Jul, 5-7 eggs, incubation 13-14 days, young fledge at 12-15 days; 1-2 broods. Hole-nester.

3   Robin

Erithacus rubecula

(Thrushes and chats)

In Britain: Jan-Dec.

Identification: 14 cm/16 g. Forehead, throat and breast bright brick-red, upperparts olive-brown. Sexes similar. Young spotted brownish. Rotund, with large dark eyes; often bobs, flicks tail, lets wings droop.

Voice: Call a very rapid *'tsiktsiktsik'*; alarm call *'tsieh'* warning of aerial predator. Song: melancholy, solemn whistling, begins with several high whistles leading to a series of clear falling rippling notes and trills.

Habitat: Woods with rich undergrowth, gardens, parks.

Food: Insects and spiders.

Breeding: Apr-Jun, 4-6 eggs, incubation 14 days, young fledge at 13-14 days; double-brooded. Nests on ground.

Bluethroat

Luscinia svecica

(Thrushes and chats)

In Britain: Scarce migrant.

Identification: 14 cm/18 g. Size of Robin (p. 202), but more slender, longer-legged, orange-red at base of tail; male with throat and upper breast shining blue with white 'star' in centre of breast (Plate). The Scandinavian race (back cover) has a red star. Female with whitish throat.

Voice: Call a hard *'tack'* or *'tk'*. Song: hurried chirping and purring phrases, with buzzing notes, mixed with whistles and mimicry.

Habitat: Dried up pools and ponds with reeds and willows; scrub tundra.

Food: Insects and spiders.

Breeding: Apr-Jun, 5-6 eggs, incubation 13 days, young fledge at 13-14 days. Nests on ground.

Nightingale

Luscinia megarhynchos

(Thrushes and chats)

In Britain: Apr-Sep.

Identification: 16.5 cm/22 g. Upperparts, wings, tail reddish-brown, underparts paler brown; long-legged. Sexes similar. Inconspicuous, remaining hidden, hops with large bounds, wags tail regularly.

Voice: When agitated a soft, plaintive *'hewid'* or a deep *'karr'*. Song: loud, very varied, with many crystal clear motifs coming thick and fast, interspersed with monotonous warbling figures, amongst which are long drawn-out crescendo notes ('jugging'); sings also at night.

Habitat: Deciduous woods, coppice, gardens, parks. *Food:* Insects and spiders.

Breeding: May-Jun, 4-6 eggs, incubation 13-14 days, young fledge at 11 days. Nests on ground.

Thrush Nightingale

Luscinia luscinia

(Thrushes and chats)

In Britain: Rare vagrant.

Identification: 16.5 cm/23 g. Very like Nightingale, but upperparts and tail olive-brown, not reddish-brown, breast clouded brownish. Wags tail in circular movement. Sexes similar.

Voice: Call when agitated like Nightingale, but deeper *'karr'* and high *'hid'*. Song: much slower in tempo than Nightingale, deeper pitched; pure bell-like notes, of one or two syllables, combined in short phrases, lacking 'jugging'; tone colour metallic. *Habitat:* Damp copses, wet woodland with alders and willow.

Food: Insects and spiders. *Breeding:* May-Jun, 4-6 eggs, incubation 13-14 days, young fledge at 11 days. Nests on ground.

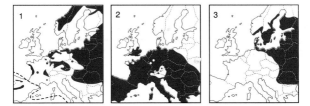

PASSERINES 2
Flight outlines and silhouettes

Swift (for comparison)

Swallow

House Martin

Sand Martin

Crested Lark

Skylark

Woodlark

Water Pipit

Meadow Pipit

Tree Pipit

Yellow Wagtail

Pied Wagtail

Grey Wagtail

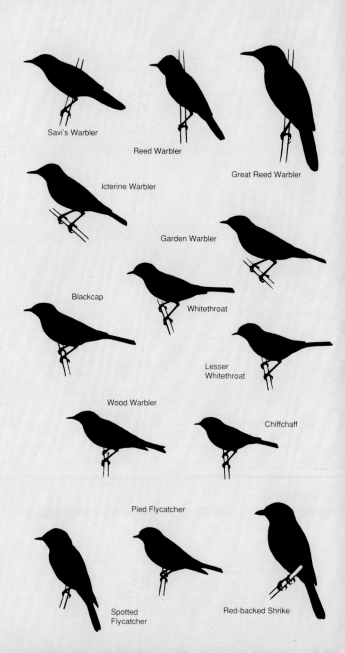

Savi's Warbler

Reed Warbler

Great Reed Warbler

Icterine Warbler

Garden Warbler

Blackcap

Whitethroat

Lesser
Whitethroat

Wood Warbler

Chiffchaff

Pied Flycatcher

Spotted
Flycatcher

Red-backed Shrike

Blackbird

Turdus merula

(Thrushes and chats)

In Britain: Jan-Dec.

Identification: 25 cm/95 g. Male jet-black with orange-yellow bill; female dark brown with lightly spotted breast. Young brown with strong spotting on underparts.

Voice: Call when agitated *'tak tak'* or very rapid *'tixtixtixtix'*; when threatened by ground predator (e.g. cat) a muted *'duk duk'*, from air (e.g. Sparrowhawk) *'tsieh'*. Song: resonant phrases of rich flute-like and mellow organ-like tone-colour.

Habitat: Woods, gardens, parks; common in villages and towns.

Food: Earthworms, insects; in autumn also berries and other fruits.

Breeding: Mar-Jul, 3-5 eggs, incubation 12-14 days, young fledge at 13 days; double-brooded. Nests in bushes and trees.

Ring Ouzel

Turdus torquatus

(Thrushes and chats)

In Britain: Apr-Oct.

Identification: 24 cm/100 g. In size and colour like Blackbird, but not so black, with white crescent-shaped breast band and white feather fringes on underparts and wings; female brownish, breast band only suggested.

Voice: Call a Blackbird-like *'tak'* or *'tocktock tock'*; in flight *'tschvierr'*. Song: structured like Song Thrush, but less musical and varied, tone quality recalls Mistle Thrush (p. 210).

Habitat: On Continent conifer woods in mountains, at the tree-line; in Britain rocky hillsides, scree.

Food: As Blackbird.

Breeding: Apr-Jul, 4-5 eggs, incubation 12-14 days, young fledge at 14-16 days; double-brooded. Nests in trees and bushes, or on rock ledge.

Fieldfare

Turdus pilaris

(Thrushes and chats)

In Britain: Oct-Apr; has bred.

Identification: 25.5 cm/100 g. Head and rump grey, back chestnut-brown, throat and breast rusty-yellow. Sexes similar. Gregarious.

Voice: Flight call *'schack-schack-schack'*; in nest defence a rasping *'trarrat'*. Song: unremarkable, short, squeezed scratchy warbling, mostly in flight.

Habitat: Birch woods, poplar avenues, copses, woodland edge, parks.

Food: Worms, snails, insects and berries.

Breeding: Apr-Jun, 5-6 eggs, incubation 11-14 days, young fledge at 14 days; sometimes double-brooded. Nests in trees in loose colonies.

1

2

3

1 # Redwing
Turdus iliacus

(Thrushes and chats)

In Britain: Sep-Apr; very small numbers breed.

Identification: 21 cm/65 g. Smaller than Song Thrush, flanks and underwing red-chestnut, cream-coloured stripe over eye and moustachial stripe. Sexes similar.

Voice: On migration and in flight a high, drawn out *'tsiieh'*. Song: series of falling whistling notes, followed by a scratching croaking warble.

Habitat: Birch woods, mixed and conifer woods.

Food: Worms, snails, insects and berries.

Breeding: May-Jul, 5-6 eggs, incubation 12-14 days, young fledge at 8-12 days; 1-2 broods a year. Nests in trees and bushes, also on the ground.

2 # Song Thrush
Turdus philomelos

(Thrushes and chats)

In Britain: Jan-Dec.

Identification: 23 cm/70 g. Smaller than Blackbird (p. 208). Upperparts dark brown, underparts whitish with dense spotting, breast creamy-buff.

Voice: When nest threatened scolds like Blackbird *'dickdickdick'*, but more muffled; in flight a short *'tsip'*. Song: musical, structured in phrases which consist of motifs repeated from two to four times such as *'judiet-judiet-judiet'*.

Habitat: Woods, parks, gardens.

Food: Mainly garden snails which it breaks open on a stone, the 'thrushes' anvil'; also worms, insects, berries.

Breeding: Mar-Jul, 3-6 eggs, incubation 12-13 days, young fledge at 14 days; double-brooded. Nests in trees and bushes.

3 # Mistle Thrush
Turdus viscivorus

(Thrushes and chats)

In Britain: Jan-Dec.

Identification: 27 cm/120 g. Largest European thrush. Upperparts grey-brown, underparts whitish with coarse spotting. Sexes similar.

Voice: In flight a hard grating *'schnirr'*. Song: Blackbird-like in tone, but shorter, melancholy, monotonous phrases, which are delivered at the same pitch.

Habitat: Mature coniferous forest up to the tree-line, mixed and deciduous woods, parkland, gardens.

Food: Worms, snails, insects; in autumn and winter mistletoe berries and windfall fruit.

Breeding: Mar-Jun, 3-5 eggs, incubation 14 days, young fledge at 12-15 days; double-brooded. Tree-nester.

Bearded Tit

Panurus biarmicus

(Babblers)

In Britain: Jan-Dec.

Identification: 16.5 cm/15 g. Plumage of male cinnamon-brown, head pale grey, black moustache, long graduated tail. Female with crown cinnamon-brown, lacking moustache. Climbs in reeds, whirring flight low over reedbeds.

Voice: Flight call a nasal *'ping-ping'*, when disturbed *'pitt'*. Song: various motifs with irregular spacing *'tschri pitt-pitt tsched driuu'*.

Habitat: Extensive reedbeds.

Food: In summer insects, in winter reed seeds.

Breeding: Apr-Jul, 5-7 eggs, incubation 12-13 days, young fledge at 10-13 days; double-brooded. Bowl-shaped nest low down among folded reed stems.

Long-tailed Tit

Aegithalos caudatus

(Long-tailed Tits)

In Britain: Jan-Dec.

Identification: 14 cm/8 g. Small, round body with very long graduated tail; head white with broad black stripe over eye (North European race with pure white head, Plate). Sexes similar. Young with sides of head dark brown. Sociable.

Voice: Calls frequently *'tschrrt'*, *'tserr'* or *'siet siet'*. Song: soft chirping and trilling.

Habitat: Deciduous and mixed woodland, copses, heathlands, gardens and parks.

Food: Insects and spiders.

Breeding: Apr-Jun, 8-10 eggs, incubation 13-16 days, young fledge at 14-16 days. Domed nest.

Penduline Tit

Remiz pendulinus

(Penduline Tits)

In Britain: Increasing vagrant.

Identification: 11 cm/10 g. Head whitish, forehead and cheeks black forming mask, back and wing coverts chestnut-brown, underparts cream-coloured; female paler; young lacking black on head. Acrobatic on thin twigs; sociable when not breeding.

Voice: Call a high soft falling *'tsieh'*. Song: short repeated elements such as *'sit'*, combined with the call.

Habitat: Copses, willow thickets by rivers and lakes.

Food: Insects and spiders; in winter also seeds.

Breeding: Apr-Jun, 6-8 eggs, incubation 12-15 days, young fledge from 20 days; double-brooded. Free-hanging feltlike pouch-shaped nest on the end of a branch.

Great Tit

Parus major

(Tits)

In Britain: Jan-Dec.

Identification: 14 cm/19 g. Head black with white cheeks, back olive-green, underparts yellow with black stripe down centre of breast; female a little paler. Confiding; acrobatic, often hops on ground.

Voice: Call *'tsituit'*, *'pink'*, when disturbed a rasping *'tscher-r-r-r'* or *'pink dedede'*. Song: repeated two to four syllable piping motif *'tsitsibeh'*, *'tsipe'* or similar.

Habitat: All types of woodland, gardens, parks.

Food: Insects, berries, seeds; common at bird-tables.

Breeding: Apr-Jul, 8-12 eggs, incubation 12-15 days, young fledge at 16-22 days; 1-2 broods. Hole-nester.

Blue Tit

Parus caeruleus

(Tits)

In Britain: Jan-Dec.

Identification: 11.5 cm/11 g. Crown blue, sides of head white with black stripe through eye, wings and tail blue, underparts yellow; female paler. Confiding; often hangs from thin twigs; short display flight on vibrating wings.

Voice: Call a rising *'tserrretetetet'* or *'tsie-tsi-tsi'*. Song: high trill *'tsie-tsi-tsirrrr'*, *'tsi-tsi-trriu-trriu'* or *'tsi-tsi-tsi-tsi'*.

Habitat: Deciduous and mixed woodland, gardens, parks.

Food: Small insects, seeds; common at bird-tables.

Breeding: Apr-Jun, 7-14 eggs, incubation 13-15 days, young fledge at 16-22 days; 1-2 broods a year (1 in Britain). Hole-nester.

Crested Tit

Parus cristatus

(Tits)

In Britain: Jan-Dec; only in Scotland.

Identification: 11.5 cm/11 g. Small brown tit with conspicuous black-and-white 'scaly' crest. Sexes similar. Sprightly acrobat, usually high in conifers.

Voice: Call a purring *'iurrr-r'* or *'tsi tsi gurrrr'*. Song: like the repeated call *'tsie tsi tsi gurrrr tsigurrrr'*.

Habitat: Conifer woodland, both lowland and upland up to tree-line, mixed woods; in southern Europe also deciduous woods.

Food: Small insects and spiders, conifer seeds; occasional at bird-tables.

Breeding: Apr-Jun, 5-8 eggs, incubation 13-15 days, young fledge at 17-21 days; 1-2 broods a year. Hole-nester.

1   Marsh Tit

Parus palustris

(Tits)

In Britain: Jan.-Dec.

Identification: 11.5 cm/11 g. Very similar to Willow Tit, but head smaller, shiny black cap, lacking pale panel in wing, smaller blacker bib; upperparts grey-brown, underparts dirty white. Sexes similar.

Voice: Call a distinctive *'pistyu'* followed by a rapid scolding *'dididi'*. Song: short repeated rattling such as *'tsietsietsie'*, *'diepdiepdiep'* or *'ti-viud-ti-viud'*.

Habitat: Deciduous woods with rich undergrowth, parkland, orchards, in mountains up to 1400 m altitude; not in marshes!

Food: Insects, seeds.

Breeding: Apr-May, 7-8 eggs, incubation 13-15 days, young fledge at 17-20 days. Hole-nester.

2   Willow Tit

Parus montanus

(Tits)

In Britain: Jan.-Dec.

Identification: 11.5 cm/11 g. Very similar to Marsh Tit, but head larger, matt black cap, pale panel in wing, bib black, extending on to throat, flanks brownish. Sexes similar.

Voice: Call an extended nasal *'deh-deh-deh'* or *'tsi-tsi-deh-deh'*. Song: repeated high-pitched clear whistling *'tsiu-tsiu-tsiu'* or *'tsie-tsie-tsie'*.

Habitat: Marshy woods with birch, alder and willow, mixed and conifer woods.

Food: Insects, seeds.

Breeding: Apr-Jun, 7-9 eggs, incubation 13-14 days, young fledge at 17-19 days. Hole-nester, often excavates own hole.

3   Coal Tit

Parus ater

(Tits)

In Britain: Jan.-Dec.

Identification: 11 cm/9 g. Similar plumage pattern to Great Tit (p. 214), but much smaller, underparts pale grey-brown; more elongated, whiter nape patch. Sexes similar.

Voice: Call a high thin *'tsi'*, *'tsiti'* or similar. Song: short phrases of two or three syllable motifs such as *'vitse-vitse-vitse'*, *'tsevi-tsi-tsevi-tsi'* or *'sitiu-diuti-diuti'*.

Habitat: Conifer woods, parks with conifers, mountain regions up to tree-line.

Food: Insects, conifer seeds.

Breeding: Apr-Jun, 8-10 eggs, incubation 14-16 days, young fledge at 18-20 days; 1-2 broods. Hole-nester.

1   Nuthatch

Sitta europaea

(Nuthatches)

In Britain: Jan-Dec.

Identification: 14 cm/23 g. Short-tailed and stocky with woodpecker-like bill; upperparts blue-grey, underparts orange-buff (white in the Scandinavian race with chestnut wash on flanks). Sexes similar. Climbs tree trunks, head down as well as up.

Voice: Call *'tuit tuituit'*, *'tviet'*, when agitated *'tsirrrr'*, contact call *'tsit'*. Song: long series of whistling notes or trills *'tew-tew-tew'*, *'vivivivi'* or *'tiurrrr'*.

Habitat: Deciduous and mixed woodland, gardens, parks.

Food: Bark-dwelling insects, seeds.

Breeding: Apr-Jun, 6-8 eggs, incubation 13-15 days, young fledge at 22-25 days. Hole-nester, plasters up entrance to nest with mud so that bird can only just enter.

2   Treecreeper

Certhia familiaris

(Treecreepers)

In Britain: Jan-Dec.

Identification: 12.5 cm/9 g. Bark-coloured, long stiff tail, long curved bill; very like Short-toed Treecreeper, but forehead spotted white, bill a little shorter, hind claw longer, upperparts spotted white (rather than streaked), underparts pure white. Sexes similar.

Voice: A high thin *'srrie'*, *'sirr'* or *'sit'*, usually repeated. Song: falling, effervescent series of notes *'sirr-uisiri-tierrrruit'*.

Habitat: Closed conifer and mixed woodland, up to the tree-line.

Food: Bark-dwelling insects.

Breeding: Apr-Jul, 4-7 eggs, incubation 13-15 days, young fledge at 14-17 days; 1-2 broods. Nests in crevice in bark.

3   Short-toed Treecreeper

Certhia brachydactyla

(Treecreepers)

In Britain: Rare vagrant.

Identification: 12.5 cm/9 g. Very like Treecreeper, but bill a little longer, hind claw shorter, upperparts streaked white, flanks brownish.

Voice: Call high and loud *'ti ti ti'*, alarm call *'tiut tiut'*. Song: rising series of high thin whistling notes *'tsi tsi tsirlui-tsi'*.

Habitat: Deciduous and mixed woodland, gardens, parks; not above 1400 m.

Food: Bark-dwelling insects.

Breeding: Apr-Jul, 5-7 eggs, incubation 13-15 days, young fledge at 16-18 days; double-brooded. Nests in crevice in bark.

1 Wallcreeper
Tichodroma muraria

(Wallcreepers)

In Britain: Rare vagrant.

Identification: 16 cm/18 g. Broad, rounded red-and-black wings with white spots, long curved bill; upperparts grey, chin and throat black; in female and winter plumage chin and throat whitish. Climbs on vertical cliff faces; flight light and butterfly-like; often descends in winter to valleys.

Voice: Call a whistling *'tui'*. Song: rising phrase of 3-5 drawn-out whistles, the last note dropping *'dih-briuh-tsieh-diuoh'* or *'uit-trie-tiuu'*.

Habitat: Cliff faces in high mountains.

Food: Insects.

Breeding: May-Jul, 3-5 eggs, incubation 18-19 days, young fledge at 28-30 days. Nests in rock crevice.

2 Dipper
Cinclus cinclus

(Dippers)

In Britain: Jan-Dec.

Identification: 18 cm/60 g. Plump, short-tailed, dark brown thrush-sized bird with large white bib across throat and breast. Sexes similar. Young spotted grey-brown. Bobs regularly; swims and dives; flight direct on whirring wings.

Voice: Call a hard *'tsitt'* or *'schrett-schrett'*. Song: chattering series of whistling and scratching notes, such as *'tsi-tsi-trriu-trriu-vitt-vitt-trriu'*.

Habitat: Fast-flowing clear waters; up to more than 2000 m altitude.

Food: Aquatic insects and their larvae, small crustaceans, worms.

Breeding: Mar-Jun, 4-5 eggs, incubation 14-17 days, young fledge at 20-24 days; double-brooded. Dome-shaped nest of moss on rock ledge or under bridge.

3 Wren
Troglodytes troglodytes

(Wrens)

In Britain: Jan-Dec.

Identification: 9.5 cm/9 g. Tiny round brown bird with short tail, often cocked; cream-coloured stripe over eye. Very sprightly; flight direct and whirring; sings from elevated perch.

Voice: Call a hard *'teck teck'*, *'tr tr'* or churring *'tserrrr'*. Song: loud warbling chirruping phrases with long rolling trill at the end.

Habitat: Undergrowth, piles of brushwood, thickets, tangles, often near water.

Food: Insects.

Breeding: Apr-Jul, 5-7 eggs, incubation 14-16 days, young fledge at 15-18 days; double-brooded. Dome-shaped nest of moss.

1 # Yellowhammer

Emberiza citrinella

(Buntings)

In Britain: Jan.-Dec.

Identification: 16.5 cm/30 g. Head and underparts bright lemon-yellow, upperparts yellowish-brown, streaked dark brown, rump cinnamon-brown. Female and young browner. Searches for food on the ground; sings from elevated perch, regularly flicks tail; in winter in small flocks.

Voice: Call *'tsrik'*, *'tsiurr'*, *'tsip-tsi-tsi'*, when taking off *'tirr-tirr'*. Song: short stereotyped rising phrase with a deeper drawn-out final note *'zizizizizizie-diuh'*.

Habitat: Open farmland, copses, railway embankments, plantations.

Food: Seeds, green plant material, insects.

Black-headed
Bunting

Breeding: Apr.-Jul., 3-5 eggs, incubation 12-13 days, young fledge at 11-14 days; double-brooded. Cup-shaped nest low in vegetation.

Similar species: **Black-headed Bunting** *Emberiza melanocephala*. Identified by its black head and pale chestnut-brown upperparts. Female and young washed-out yellow, without obvious cap. Male sings a short melodious phrase consisting of accelerating notes of different pitch from an elevated perch. The Black-headed Bunting inhabits open countryside with trees and bushes, orchards and vineyards in southeast Europe; only from May to July in breeding area.

2 # Corn Bunting

Miliaria calandra

(Buntings)

In Britain: Jan.-Dec.

Identification: 18 cm/50 g. Largest European bunting, plump, stocky bird with very stout bill; inconspicuously coloured like a lark, wings and tail without white. Sexes similar. Searches for food on the ground; sings from elevated perch; flight whirring, often with legs dangling; in winter in flocks.

Voice: Call *'tsick tsick'*, when agitated *'tsri tsri'*, contact call *'slib'*. Song: a short stereotyped phrase which begins with accelerating notes and ends in a shrill jangling, such as *'tsick tsick tsick-tsickschnirrrp'*.

Habitat: Open, dry farmland and grassland with isolated trees and bushes, especially in warmer regions.

Food: Seeds, green plant material, insects.

Breeding: May-Aug., 3-5 eggs, incubation 12-14 days, young fledge at 9-14 days; 1-2 broods a year. Nests on ground.

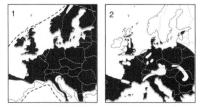

1

2

1 Lapland Bunting
Calcarius lapponicus

(Buntings)

In Britain: Sep-Apr; winter visitor mainly to North Sea coasts; has bred.
Identification: 15 cm/24 g. Head and throat black, whitish stripe behind eye, bill yellow; upperparts reddish-brown, streaked black. Female and winter plumage birds with streaked brown head, chin and throat whitish.
Voice: Call *'tiuu'*, in flight a trilling *'tititi'*. Song: short Skylark-like phrases.
Habitat: Low-lying and mountain tundra; in winter often in coastal fields.
Food: Seeds, insects.
Breeding: May-Jun, 4-5 eggs, incubation 13-14 days, young fledge at 10-12 days. Nests on ground.

2 Reed Bunting
Emberiza schoeniclus

(Buntings)

In Britain: Jan-Dec.
Identification: 15 cm/20 g. Head, bill and throat black, white moustachial stripe, upperparts reddish-brown, striped black. In winter head and throat grey-brown. Female and young with brown head, black-and-white moustachial stripes, pale stripe over eye, throat whitish. Sings from reed tops; flicks tail.
Voice: Call a sharp drawn-out falling *'tsieh'*. Song: short stammering phrase *'tsie tsie tsie tui tsirri'*.
Habitat: Silted up areas and river banks with reeds and willow scrub, marshy areas, scrub tundra.
Food: Seeds, insects.
Breeding: May-Jul, 4-6 eggs, incubation 12-14 days, young fledge at 10-13 days; double-brooded. Cup-shaped nest close to ground.

3 Ortolan Bunting
Emberiza hortulana

(Buntings)

In Britain: Aug-Oct; scarce migrant.
Identification: 16.5 cm/25 g. Head grey, moustachial stripe, chin and throat yellowish, yellowish eye-ring; upperparts and rump brown, underparts cinnamon-brown. Female and young paler, streaked darker on crown and breast. Sings from elevated perch.
Voice: Call *'tsia'* or *'tsie'*. Song: short Yellowhammer-like phrase with melancholy tone *'yif yif yif yif yif tiur tiur'*.
Habitat: Open, dry countryside, farmland with isolated trees and bushes, bushy steppe, maquis; up to more than 2000 m altitude.
Food: Seeds, insects. *Breeding:* May-Jul, 4-6 eggs, incubation 13 days, young fledge at 9-13 days. Cup-shaped nest close to ground.

Snow Bunting

Plectrophenax nivalis

(Buntings)

In Britain: Jan-Dec; rare breeding bird.

Identification: 16.5 cm/35 g. In summer plumage sharply contrasting black-and-white (Plate 1). Female and young with upperparts washed grey, underparts dirty white. In winter dress (Plate 2) head sandy-buff, upperparts streaked brownish, underparts cream-coloured. Female with smaller white patch in wing. Often sings in song flight.

Voice: Call a tinkling *'birrr'*, *'diuu'* or *'tsrr'*. Song: short, lark-like trilling phrase.

Habitat: Barren, stony tundra, rocky coasts, rocky mountains; also human settlements; in winter often in flocks on the North Sea and Baltic coasts.

Food: Seeds, insects.

Breeding: May-Jul, 5-6 eggs, incubation 12-14 days, young fledge at 10-14 days. Nests in hole in rock.

Rock Bunting

Emberiza cia

(Buntings)

In Britain: Rare vagrant.

Identification: 16 cm/25 g. Head ash-grey with black stripes, belly cinnamon-brown, upperparts cinnamon, streaked darker. Female and young duller. Sings from elevated perch; often spreads tail.

Voice: Call a high *'tsip'* or *'tsihp'*. Song: short, high-pitched hurried phrase, recalling Dunnock.

Habitat: Sunny rocky hillsides, vineyards. *Food:* Seeds, insects.

Breeding: May-Jul, 3-5 eggs, incubation 12-13 days, young fledge at 10-13 days; 1-2 broods a year. Cup-shaped nest, usually on ground.

Cirl Bunting

Emberiza cirlus

(Buntings)

In Britain: Jan-Dec.

Identification: 16.5 cm/25 g. Head striped black and yellow, chin and throat black, rump olive-brown; in winter throat grey. Female and young lacking conspicuous head pattern. Sings from elevated perch.

Voice: Call a high *'tsieh'* or *'tsip'*. Song: short rattling phrase *'tzetzetzetzetze'*, similar to the rattle of Lesser Whitethroat.

Habitat: Open countryside with isolated trees and bushes, woodland edge, hillsides; warmth-loving; in the south also open oakwoods, maquis and vineyards.

Food: Insects, seeds.

Breeding: May-Aug, 3-5 eggs, incubation 12-13 days, young fledge at 10-13 days; double-brooded. Nests close to ground.

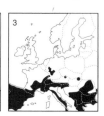

Chaffinch

Fringilla coelebs

(Finches)

In Britain: Jan-Dec.

Identification: 15 cm/22 g. Male (Plate 1) with crown, nape and bill blue-grey, underparts reddish-brown, two white wingbars, outer tail feathers white, rump olive-green. Female (Plate 2) and young with upperparts olive-brown, underparts pale. Hops along the ground with jerky head movements.

Voice: Call *'pink'*, soft *'fuid'* or *'trriub'*, in flight *'chup'*. Song: loud warbling phrase such as *'tsitsitsitsietsie tsiatsiatsia-tsoritiu-kick'*.

Habitat: Woods, copses, gardens and parks. *Food:* Insects, seeds.

Breeding: Apr-Jul, 3-6 eggs, incubation 11-13 days, young fledge at 13-14 days. Nests in trees.

Brambling

Fringilla montifringilla

(Finches)

In Britain: Oct-Apr; has bred.

Identification: 15 cm/25 g. Male with breast and shoulders orange, head and back black, rump white. Female and male winter plumage (Plate 3) duller, head and back scaled brownish. In winter in large flocks in beech woods.

Voice: Call a squawking *'queih'*, in flight *'chukchuk'*. Song: rattling with harsh drawn-out squawking notes. *Habitat:* Deciduous, mixed and conifer woods.

Food: Insects, seeds, especially beechmast.

Breeding: May-Jul, 5-7 eggs, incubation 13 days, young fledge at 12-14 days. Nests in trees.

Crossbill

Loxia curvirostra

(Finches)

In Britain: Jan-Dec.

Identification: 16.5 cm/40 g. Brick-red, stocky finch with mandibles crossed at tip. Female olive-green. Sociable; clambers acrobatically on conifer branches after cones.

Voice: Flight call a hard *'kipp kipp'*. Song: whistling and jangling phrases, mixed with flight calls.

Habitat: Spruce and fir woods, especially in mountains. *Food:* Conifer seeds.

Breeding: Timed to coincide with availability of food, usually Feb-May, 3-4 eggs, incubation 12-16 days, young fledge at 20-25 days; 1-2 broods a year. Nests in conifer.

Similar species: **Parrot Crossbill** *Loxia pytyopsittacus*. Somewhat larger and with more powerful bill than Crossbill. Call rather deeper; in pine forests of northern Europe; occasional invasions further south into Europe.

Scottish Crossbill *Loxia scotica*

(Finches)

In Britain: Jan-Dec; the only species of bird unique to Britain.
Identification: 17 cm/40 g. Very similar to Crossbill. Differs only in its
bill, which is deeper, stouter.
Voice: Similar to Crossbill, though more varied; deep *'toop'* said to be diagnostic.
Habitat: Restricted to Caledonian pine forest.
Food: Mainly seeds of Scots Pine; also other tree seeds.
Breeding: Mar-Jun, 3-4 eggs, incubation 13-15 days, young fledge at 17-20 days.

Scarlet Rosefinch *Carpodacus erythrinus*

(Finches)

In Britain: May-Oct; rare, increasing.
Identification: 14.5 cm/21 g. Head, breast and rump carmine-red,
upperparts brown, belly reddish-cream. Female brownish, lacking red.
Flight undulating.
Voice: Call *'tslit'* and a squeezed *'tschiui'*, when threatened a hoarse *'rrii'*.
Song: short, oriole-like whistling phrase *'diu-diu-di-diuidyu'*.
Habitat: Damp habitats with birch, alder, willow scrub; riverside bushes,
open mixed woods, parkland.
Food: Buds, seeds, insects.
Breeding: Jun-Jul, 4-6 eggs, incubation 12-14 days, young fledge at
12-16 days. Nests in bushes.

Bullfinch *Pyrrhula pyrrhula*

(Finches)

In Britain: Jan-Dec.
Identification: 15 cm/24 g. Stocky with black cap; upperparts blue-grey,
wings black with white bar, rump gleaming white; underparts and cheeks
in male bright rose-red, in female pinkish-grey. Young brownish, lacking
black cap. Not shy; mostly in pairs or family groups, in winter often in
small flocks.
Voice: Call melancholy, soft, falling *'diuu'* or *'viup'*, contact call a soft
'bit-bit'. Song: soft hollow series of piping and squeezed notes.
Habitat: Conifer and mixed woods, parks, gardens and orchards.
Food: Seeds, berries, buds, insects.
Breeding: May-Aug, 4-6 eggs, incubation 13 days, young fledge at
12-16 days; 2-3 broods a year. Nests in trees, bushes.

1 Greenfinch
Carduelis chloris

(Finches)

In Britain: Jan.-Dec.

Identification: 14.5 cm/30 g. Yellow-green finch with yellow in wing and at base of tail. Female grey-green. Young streaked dark. Sings from elevated perch or in bat-like song flight.

Voice: Call *'diui'*, in flight a ringing *'giugiugiu'*. Song: trilling and ringing phrases, interspersed with drawn-out nasal *'tsweee'* notes.

Habitat: Open mixed woods, copses, parks, gardens, avenues.

Food: Seeds, buds, berries; often on bird-tables.

Breeding: Apr-Aug, 4-6 eggs, incubation 13 days, young fledge at 13-16 days; 2-3 broods a year. Nests in conifers and bushes.

2 Goldfinch
Carduelis carduelis

(Finches)

In Britain: Jan.-Dec.

Identification: 12 cm/16 g. Black-and-white head with bright red mask and gleaming yellow wing bar. Sexes similar. Young grey-brown, lacking red on head, underparts streaked. In autumn and winter in small flocks.

Voice: Call a ringing *'didlit'*, also given in flight. Song: lively twittering with scattered call- and *'tserr'*-notes.

Habitat: Orchards, villages, gardens, parks, avenues.

Food: Thistle, dandelion and tree seeds, aphids.

Breeding: May-Aug, 4-6 eggs, incubation 13 days, young fledge at 13-15 days; double-brooded. Nests in trees.

3 Siskin
Carduelis spinus

(Finches)

In Britain: Jan.-Dec.

Identification: 12 cm/12 g. Small yellow-green finch with black crown; wings black with yellow-green bars and patch. Female grey-green, crown greyer, underparts streaked black. Young with upperparts strongly streaked as well. Bat-like song flight.

Voice: Flight call a hoarse *'tsiiuh'*, contact call *'tettettett'*. Song: short, hurried twittering phrases with long drawn-out chattering ending.

Habitat: Spruce and mixed woods, parks; up to 1800 m altitude.

Food: Seeds of composites, conifers, alder and birch, insects.

Breeding: Apr-Jul, 4-6 eggs, incubation 12-13 days, young fledge at 13-15 days; double-brooded. Nests in trees.

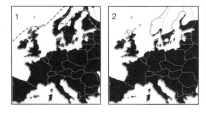

1

2

3

1 Serin

Serinus serinus

(Finches)

In Britain: Apr-Oct; scarce visitor.

Identification: 11.5 cm/12 g. Very small, head, throat and breast yellow, cheeks and nape greyish-brown, upperparts and flanks streaked darker, yellow rump. Female and young grey-green, streaked underparts. Sings from elevated perch or in bat-like song flight.

Voice: Call trilling *'trititititiu'*, when threatened a drawn-out *'trui'*, in flight *'girlitt'*. Song: continuous tinkling twittering on more or less the same pitch.

Habitat: Open deciduous and mixed woodland, gardens, parks, vineyards.

Food: Seeds, green plant material.

Breeding: Apr-Jul, 3-5 eggs, incubation 13 days, young fledge at 14-16 days; double-brooded. Nests in trees.

2 Redpoll

Carduelis flammea

(Finches)

In Britain: Jan-Dec.

Identification: 13 cm/12 g. Similar to Linnet (p. 236) but forehead and chin black, upperparts and flanks streaked dark, crown red, breast with reddish flush. Female lacking red on breast; young brownish. Often sings in flight. In winter sociable.

Voice: Call nasal *'dsei'*, in flight *'dschedschedsche'*. Song: continuous twittering of ringing and buzzing phrases *'irr chichichi dschrrr dschedsche'*.

Habitat: Scrub tundra, conifer woods, birch, alder and willow copses; in the Alps, mainly near the tree-line.

Food: Seeds, insects.

Breeding: May-Jul, 4-6 eggs, incubation 11-13 days, young fledge at 12 days. Nests in trees.

3 Citril Finch

Serinus citrinella

(Finches)

In Britain: Very rare vagrant: 1 record.

Identification: 12 cm/15 g. Small, unstreaked; face and underparts yellow, nape, cheeks, sides of neck grey. Female greenish-grey; young streaked.

Voice: In flight nasal *'di di'*, *'dedlidede'*. Song: Serin-like but not so high-pitched, with drawn-out nasal notes.

Habitat: Open mountain conifer woods towards the tree-line; in winter in valleys.

Food: Conifer, weed and grass seeds, insects.

Breeding: May-Aug, 4-5 eggs, incubation 13 days, young fledge at 17-18 days; double-brooded. Nests in trees.

Linnet

Carduelis cannabina

(Finches)

In Britain: Jan-Dec.

Identification: 13.5 cm/19 g. Fore-crown and breast red, chin whitish, back red-brown. In winter only breast remains pale reddish. Female and young lacking red, streaked dark brown. Sociable; in winter in flocks.

Voice: Flight call *'gegege'*, alarm call nasal *'dieh'* or *'dliuh'*. Song: melodious, nasal twittering.

Habitat: Farmland with hedges and copses, heathland, gardens, parks.

Food: Seeds.

Breeding: Apr-Aug, 4-6 eggs, incubation 12-13 days, young fledge at 11-16 days; 2-3 broods a year. Nests in bushes, usually in loose colonies.

Hawfinch

Coccothraustes coccothraustes

(Finches)

In Britain: Jan-Dec.

Identification: 18 cm/55 g. Large, stocky and short-tailed, with huge blue-grey bill; in flight white wingbars and tail band conspicuous. Female paler. In winter bill yellowish. Usually high in trees; sociable; in winter in flocks.

Voice: Call sharp *'tsicks'*, *'tsittitt'* or *'tsieh'*. Song: stammering jangle with hollow repeated call-notes.

Habitat: Deciduous and mixed woods, parks and gardens.

Food: Cherry stones, seeds of deciduous trees, insects; on the Continent often at bird-tables.

Breeding: Apr-Jun, 4-6 eggs, incubation 11-13 days, young fledge at 11-14 days; 1-2 broods a year (1 in Britain). Nests in trees.

Snowfinch

Montifringilla nivalis

(Sparrows)

In Britain: Not recorded.

Identification: 18 cm/40 g. Head grey, bill, chin and throat black, large white wing patches, tail white with black central tail feathers. In winter plumage (Plate) and female, throat spotted white, bill yellow. Sings from the ground or in song flight; flicks tail.

Voice: Call a squawking *'que'* or *'tsiih'*, in flight *'chiub'* or *'dididi'*. Song: chirping of repeated motifs like *'bitse'*, *'sittitsche'*, *'tviyu'*.

Habitat: Mountains above the tree-line.

Food: Seeds, insects.

Breeding: May-Jul, 4-6 eggs, incubation 13-14 days, young fledge at 18-21 days. Nests in small colonies in holes in rocks.

1

2

3

Twite

Carduelis flavirostris

(Finches)

In Britain: Jan-Dec.

Identification: 13.5 cm/18 g. Like dark Linnet, but slightly smaller with relatively longer tail. In winter orange-buff face and throat, pale bill; heavily streaked; male with pink rump. Sociable.

Voice: Chattering song, including diagnostic call note, a harsh nasal *'chwee'*.

Habitat: Moorland; in winter saltmarshes, coastal fields.

Food: Seeds.

Breeding: May-Jun, 5-6 eggs, incubation 12-13 days, young fledge at 15 days; double-brooded.

House Sparrow

Passer domesticus

(Sparrows)

In Britain: Jan-Dec.

Identification: 15 cm/30 g. Crown grey, bordered red-brown at the sides, cheeks whitish-grey, extensive black bib extending on to upper breast. Female plain grey-brown. Young like female. The male courts the female with loud chirping, feathers puffed up and with drooping wings and cocked tail. Very sociable; hops on the ground.

Voice: Chirping calls and clamouring *'tetetet'*. Song: garrulous, chirping chatter *'tschilp-tschelp-tschilip'*.

Habitat: Towns and villages.

Food: Buds, seeds, berries, insects, scraps.

Breeding: Apr-Aug, 3-6 eggs, incubation 12-14 days, young fledge at 13-19 days; 3-4 broods a year. Colonial breeder, mostly in holes in buildings.

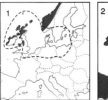

Rock Sparrow

1

Petronia petronia

(Sparrows)

In Britain: Very rare vagrant: 1 record.

Identification: 14 cm/35 g. Inconspicuous grey-brown, streaked, similar to female House Sparrow, but stockier, shorter-tailed with stouter bill and yellow spot on throat; tail feathers with white spots. Sexes similar.

Voice: Call a nasal croaking *'veih'*, clamouring *'errr'*. Song: loose series of nasal croaking, mostly disyllabic notes.

Habitat: Sunny rock faces, ruins, settlements. *Food:* Seeds, insects.

Breeding: Apr-Jun, 4-7 eggs, incubation 12-14 days, young fledge at 20-21 days; double-brooded. Colonial breeder. Nests mostly in holes in rocks or in walls.

Tree Sparrow

2

Passer montanus

(Sparrows)

In Britain: Jan-Dec.

Identification: 14 cm/23 g. Crown chestnut-brown, cheeks white with black spot, small black bib. Sexes similar. Sociable; flight more agile than House Sparrow.

Voice: Call a hard *'tschick-tschick-tschock'*, flight call *'teckteckteck'*. Song: stammering series of chirping motifs.

Habitat: Open countryside with trees, copses, edges of towns, gardens, parks. *Food:* Seeds, insects.

Breeding: Apr-Jul, 4-6 eggs, incubation 12-14 days, young fledge at 12-14 days; 2-3 broods a year. Nests in holes, also in nestboxes, seldom in buildings.

Golden Oriole

3

Oriolus oriolus

(Orioles)

In Britain: May-Sep; scarce.

Identification: 24 cm/70 g. Thrush-like; male with head, back and underparts dazzling yellow, wings, tail and lores black, bill reddish (on right of Plate). Female with upperparts yellow-green, underparts pale grey, streaked dark, wings and tail brown-black (on left of Plate). Young similar to female, but upperparts spotted. Males do not become bright yellow until their third year; old females more yellow than green, but less gleaming than the males, duller. Very rarely on the ground; rapid flier.

Voice: When disturbed a squealing *'krrii'* or *'gvii'*. Song: loud, melodious whistling *'didiualiuo'* or *'diudlioh'*.

Habitat: Poplar plantations, open deciduous woodland, extensive parkland, orchards, pine woods. *Food:* Insects, berries, fruit.

Breeding: May-Jul, 3-5 eggs, incubation 14-15 days, young fledge at 14-15 days. Hanging bowl-shaped nest in fork of branches.

1|2

3

1 Starling   *Sturnus vulgaris*
(Starlings)

In Britain: Jan-Dec.
Identification: 21.5 cm/75 g. Smaller and shorter-tailed than Blackbird (p.
208); black, green and violet glossed feathers, from autumn to spring
strongly spotted white; bill yellow, in winter dark; in flight triangular
pointed wings. Sexes similar. Young grey-brown. Sociable, often in huge
flocks; usually searches for food on the ground.
Voice: Call a shrill *'schrien'*, alarm call a hard *'spett-spett'*, *'rrih'* or hissing
'bkhrr'. Song: very varied consisting of whistling, clicking, chattering and
purring noises, mixed with a good deal of mimicry of other birds.
Habitat: Deciduous and mixed woods, copses, parks and gardens.
Food: Insects, worms, snails, cherries, grapes and other fruit.
Breeding: Apr-Jul, 4-7 eggs, incubation 12-14 days, young fledge at 18-22
days; 1-2 broods a year (usually 1 in Britain). Hole-nester, especially in
old woodpecker holes and nestboxes.

2 Nutcracker   *Nucifraga caryocatactes*
(Crows)

In Britain: Irregular vagrant.
Identification: 32 cm/170 g. Slim, with powerful, long black bill; plumage
dark chocolate-brown with white tear-shaped spots, undertail coverts
gleaming white. Sexes similar. Often sits on top of trees.
Voice: Call a loud grating *'griirr griirr'*, *'chek chek chek'*; also chattering.
Habitat: Conifer and mixed woods of upland and mountain regions; taiga.
Food: Conifer seeds, beechmast, nuts, insects.
Breeding: Mar-May, 3-4 eggs, incubation 16-21 days, young fledge at
21-25 days. Nests in trees.

3 Jay   *Garrulus glandarius*
(Crows)

In Britain: Jan-Dec.
Identification: 34 cm/170 g. Pale reddish-brown with blue-and-black
barred markings on wing, rump and undertail coverts white, tail black.
Sexes similar. Hides acorns and beechmast as winter provisions.
Voice: Call a soft *'ga-hi'*, alarm call loud screeching *'rrih-rrih'*, *'rretsch'*.
Habitat: All types of woodland up to 1600 m altitude; parkland, gardens with trees.
Food: Acorns, beechmast, fruits, insects, birds' eggs, young birds.
Breeding: Apr-Jun, 5-6 eggs, incubation 16-17 days, young fledge at 19-20
days. Nests in trees.

1 Magpie
Pica pica
(Crows)

In Britain: Jan-Dec.
Identification: 46 cm/210 g. Black-and-white corvid with very long
graduated tail; wings glossed blue, tail glossed green. Sexes similar.
Young with shorter tail and matt plumage. Flies with irregular wingbeats;
wary; outside the breeding season often in flocks.
Voice: Call a harsh *'schackackack'*, *'tscharr-ackackack'*, high *'checkcheck'*.
Song: subdued chattering with croaking and nasal notes.
Habitat: Open farmland, copses, gardens, parks.
Food: Worms, snails, insects, eggs, young birds.
Breeding: Mar-May, 5-8 eggs, incubation 17-18 days, young fledge at
22-27 days. Large nest in trees, bushes.

2 Alpine Chough
Pyrrhocorax graculus
(Crows)

In Britain: Not recorded.
Identification: 38 cm/230 g. A little larger and slimmer than Jackdaw
(p. 246), with more slender, gently curved yellow bill, legs orange-red;
plumage uniform glossy black. Sexes similar. Sociable; often glides and
soars in flocks; performs aerobatics; not shy, visits mountain huts, well
frequented mountain peaks, takes food from man.
Voice: Call sharp and shrill *'tsya'*, *'tschrirr'*, contact call *'priuit'*.
Habitat: High mountains, in winter also in valleys.
Food: Insects, worms, snails, fruits, carrion, scraps.
Breeding: Apr-Jul, 4-5 eggs, incubation 18-21 days, young fledge at
31-38 days. Nests in crevice on cliff, often in colonies.

3 Chough
Pyrrhocorax pyrrhocorax
(Crows)

In Britain: Jan-Dec.
Identification: 40 cm/300 g. Very similar to Alpine Chough, but a little
bigger, bill orange-red and much longer; plumage black with blue gloss.
Sexes similar. Magnificent flier; in display performs skilful aerobatics.
Voice: Often repeated calls such as *'pierr'*, *'kiyar'*, *'khrii'*.
Habitat: High mountains with precipitous cliffs, rocky coasts; in winter
also valleys.
Food: Insects, worms, snails, seeds, berries.
Breeding: Apr-Jun, 3-6 eggs, incubation 17-23 days, young fledge at
37-40 days. Colonial breeder.

1 Jackdaw

Corvus monedula

(Crows)

In Britain: Jan-Dec.

Identification: 33 cm/240 g. Pigeon-sized grey and black crow; upperparts black with blue gloss, nape and ear-coverts grey; iris pale blue. Sexes similar. Young with slight brownish cast. Flight more agile than the larger crows; very sociable, often in mixed flocks with Rooks; usually feeds in flocks on the ground in open countryside.

Voice: Call sonorous high *'kiack'* or *'kya'*, grating *'kierr'*, when danger threatens a high *'chiup'*. Song: series of soft chattering noises such as *'gyau-gyu'*.

Habitat: Parkland and copses with old trees, church towers, ruins, cliffs; also in deciduous woodland with tree holes.

Food: Insects, worms, snails, mice, berries, seeds, scraps.

Breeding: Apr-Jun, 4-6 eggs, incubation 17-18 days, young fledge at 28-35 days. Colonial breeder; nests in buildings, tree- or rock-holes.

2 Rook

Corvus frugilegus

(Crows)

In Britain: Jan-Dec.

Identification: 46 cm/480 g. Similar to Carrion Crow (p. 248), but with stronger blue gloss to black plumage, crown more peaked; longer, slimmer bill, unfeathered skin at base of bill whitish, belly and thigh feathers loose. Sexes similar. Young with black feathered base to bill. Wingbeats quicker than in Carrion Crow. In winter often in very large flocks in meadows, fields and in towns; in evening fly together to traditional roosts.

Voice: Deeper and rougher than Carrion Crow, *'kroh'*, *'korr'*, *'krah'*, *'gag'*, Jackdaw-like *'kiu'*. Song: croaking and chattering phrases.

Habitat: Deciduous and conifer woods, usually at the edge of open countryside, especially farmland with copses.

young

adult

Food: Beetle larvae, caterpillars, wire-worms, snails, mice, seeds, grain.

Breeding: Mar-May, 3-6 eggs, incubation 17-20 days, young fledge at 28-35 days. Colonial breeder. Nest of twigs, grass stems, earth, several together in tops of trees ('rookeries').

1 Carrion Crow

Corvus corone corone

(Crows)

In Britain: Jan-Dec.

Identification: 47 cm/550 g. Stocky and powerful, with strong black bill; plumage jet-black with weak gloss. Sexes similar, Young duller. Mostly solitary or in pairs; flies with slow regular wingbeats; soars rarely.

Voice: Call 'verr', 'kreh', 'krah', 'konk', usually repeated several times; short 'krrrkrrr' when mobbing birds of prey. Song: soft ventriloquial chattering.

Habitat: Open farmland, uplands, woods, parks, villages, towns, sea coasts.

Food: Worms, insects, small vertebrates, fruits, seeds, carrion, scraps, eggs and young birds.

Breeding: Mar-Jun, 3-6 eggs, incubation 17-20 days, young fledge at 31-32 days. Twig nest in trees.

2 Hooded Crow

Corvus corone cornix

(Crows)

In Britain: Jan-Dec.

Identification: Like Carrion Crow, but nape, back and underparts pale grey.

Voice, Habitat, Food, Breeding: As for Carrion Crow. Hooded Crow and Carrion Crow are distinctively coloured races of the same species, which hybridise in their contact zone. Such 'mixed marriages' produce fertile young, which can look like either parent or be intermediate.

3 Raven

Corvus corax

(Crows)

In Britain: Jan-Dec.

Identification: 64 cm/1.25 kg. Very similar to Carrion Crow, but distinctly larger, with very powerful bill; plumage jet-black, with blue gloss. Sexes similar. In flight longer neck and distinctive wedge-shaped tail; often soars; during display performs aerobatics.

Voice: In flight a repeated deep and sonorous 'krok', 'kroa' or 'kark'; a hollow 'klong', wooden 'kuk', crow-like 'verr'. Song: soft, ventriloquial chattering, with mimicry.

Habitat: Very varied; open deciduous and conifer woods, mountains, scrub country, steppes, rocky coasts, Arctic tundra.

Food: Very varied; insects, worms, snails, small vertebrates, seeds, fruits, carrion, scraps.

Breeding: Feb-May, 3-6 eggs, incubation 20-21 days, young fledge at about 40 days. Huge twig nest.

INDEX

Collins Nature
Guides

To order your copies please call our
24-hour credit card hotline 0141 772 2281

HarperCollins*Publishers*

PASSERINES 3
Bird Silhouettes

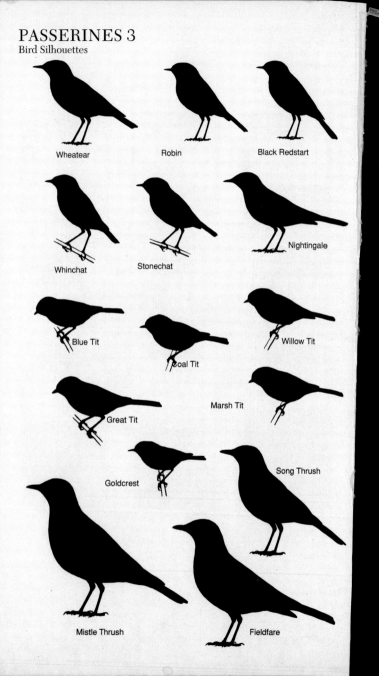

Wheatear

Robin

Black Redstart

Whinchat

Stonechat

Nightingale

Blue Tit

Coal Tit

Willow Tit

Great Tit

Marsh Tit

Goldcrest

Song Thrush

Mistle Thrush

Fieldfare